Praise for Scott Bradfield

"The most original voice of the new generation of Californian writers." *Brian Moore*

"Painfully beautiful writing." *Mary Gaitskill*

"Bradfield is one of my favorite living writers." *Jonathan Lethem*

"A wizardly writer of stories. His prose is so lucid and exact, his narrative sense so confident, that you hardly know where he's taking you until you're there." *Tobias Wolff*

"Scott Bradfield has been writing some of the wisest and funniest fiction for a while now." Sam Lipsyte

"A howlingly funny, too-neglected American writer." *The Believer*

"Scott Bradfield has not simply staked out new literary terrain… he has mapped and colonized an entire new planet." *Michael Chabon*

"A writer with a gift for characterization, as well as a delightfully wild imagination." *Stephen Amidon*

Books by Scott Bradfield:

Fiction:

The History of Luminous Motion (1989)
Dream of the Wolf: Stories (1990)
What's Wrong with America (1994)
Animal Planet (1995)
Greetings From Earth: New and Collected Stories (1996)
Good Girl Wants it Bad (2004)
Hot Animal Love: Tales of Modern Romance (2005)
The People Who Watched Her Pass By (2010)
Dazzle Resplendent: Adventures of a Misanthropic Dog (2016)

Criticism:

Dreaming Revolution (1993)
Confessions of an Unrepentant Short Story Writer (2012)
Why I Hate Toni Morrison's Beloved: *Several Decades of Reading Unwisely* (2013)

Why I Hate Toni Morrison's *Beloved*

Several Decades of Reading Unwisely

Essays & Reviews 1986 – 2013

SCOTT BRADFIELD

London: Red Rabbit Books, 2016

DEDICATION

For Ji, Jack and Mysty, my most significant critics

CONTENTS

ACKNOWLEDGMENTS

Over the decades, a few good and dependable editors prevented me (I hope) from looking like a complete idiot. Those trustworthy editors include: Alida Becker, Gregory Cowles, Robert Winder, Anthony Lane, Susan Jeffries, Ed Park, and a special thanks to Paul Maliszewski.

Introduction

WHAT I MOST fondly recall about the heyday of my book-reviewing—roughly from the late 80s through the early 2000s—is that it made me feel connected to the wide world of Literature that had never previously seemed accessible to me. The postman was regularly knocking on my door with jiffy-bagged review copies of freshly-minted books from Faber and Faber, Jonathan Cape, Picador, you name it. The phone rang every few days or so, offering me commissions for books I never heard of, or invitations to attend launch parties with a charming, shabby collection of fellow hacks and literary strivers—and sometimes, when I was lucky, I even met the occasional pretty publicity girl. Reviewing is a good part-time occupation for a writer because it gets you out of your head for several hours each day, and helps you stop worrying about the endless complexities of getting your latest fictional pages just right. Instead, you can worry about simpler things, such as getting it done on time, and within the already-prescribed limits of length.

And while my novels and stories often took years to finish, revise, sell and publish, reviews were usually accepted, copy-edited and printed within days of delivering them (often by hand) to their editors in Fleet Street, Wapping, or City Road. (They moved around quite a bit in those days). Reviewing didn't always pay well, but it almost always paid. And relatively quickly.

It was an opportunity that should probably never have happened if the Powers That Be presided over a more sensible and efficient universe of critical production. I had no idea what a book review was when I moved to London in the mid eighties, and my first review–a nasty hatchet job on a science fiction novel for *Foundation* editor, John Clute, occurred simply because I was crashing at John's Camden Town flat (as writers often do) and he needed to get a tricky book off his hands. Later, in the summer of 1987, I was staying at my friend Colin Greenland's house in Chadwell Heath, and an editor at *City Limits* (the hipper, shaggier alternative to *Time Out* in those days) called to say she had several science-fiction books to include in Colin's monthly roundup. Since Colin was unreachable (and I was, as usual, broke), I blurted: "Colin's not back for a few months. But *I'll* do them."

Miraculously, she sent me fifteen or so SF novels by bike messenger, most of which were terrible; and after a few boozy nights reading through them at a local pub, I reviewed six in fifteen hundred words or so. The review was cut to thirteen hundred words, published, I was paid, and for the next two years I became the *City Limits* SF reviewer. (Colin quite happily moved on to better things). I recall my first check from *City Limits* was meticulously worked out at something like sixty three pounds and fifty pence. And while those early reviews were clumsy and terribly written, they taught me two important lessons– one: review editors are desperate to dispose of the rapidly increasing piles of books on their desks as soon as possible, and don't mind too much who takes them. And two: your copy can be crap, but if you deliver on time, they will probably commission you again.

Not only did British literary editors answer their own phones in those days, but even when they didn't answer, their bright, usually pretty female assistants would answer and say something chipper like, "Oh yes, he's right here" and pass you on. Trying to impress them, I would blather things like, "Hi, I'm very clever and I can cover all sorts of interesting topics, such as contemporary culture, literary criticism, American politics, etcetera, etcetera," but well before my droning-on got too out of hand the chipper editor would pop back, "Hey, you're an American. Why don't I send you some American books?" And, weirdly enough, they actually did send me some American books. And when I reviewed them by deadline, they sent more.

Probably my best professional relationship was with the editors of *The Independent* during the nineties: Robert Winder (who went off to become deputy editor at *Granta* and then to write his own books) and his assistant, Anthony Lane (who went off to become a movie critic at *The New Yorker*). They were the first editors who actually commissioned me to do jobs that I asked to do—such as interview the then too-sadly-neglected Richard Yates, or to discuss my lifelong passions for subjects as diverse as the great jazz-saxophonist Art Pepper, or the thrillers of Donald E. Westlake/Richard Stark, or the brilliantly funny books and poems of that great genre-bounder, Thomas M. Disch.

For while writing about books is a difficult profession, the individual book review can often prove a stubbornly beautiful little work of art; and eventually, I learned to love the form as, I hope, I developed a few skills at the craft. Finding that first paragraph was always the bitch; but when the first paragraph did eventually arrive (often just as I was assuring my anxious editor on the phone, "Hey, it's finished and I'm heading for the tube rightthisminute!") the rest of the piece could be surprisingly fun to compose, polish and deliver. I still remember happily reading many of these pieces for the first time in their published form, often over a morning fry-up at my local cafe on Finsbury Park Road. They make me proud to have written them, and equally proud to have recovered them from the print-smeared bin of journalistic history.

If nothing else, they record what the literary world looked like to me over the last few decades or so, and they record it with as much honesty and art as I could muster.

– London, July 2013

I.

Hating and/or Loving

SCOTT BRADFIELD

Why I Hate Toni Morrison's *Beloved*

THE FIRST TIME I told someone that I had problems reading Toni Morrison's *Beloved*, she started yelling at me in a Marie Callender's restaurant in Dana Point, California. I had recently received my Ph.D in English at UC Irvine, just a dozen miles northwards, and we were having what graduate students consider a "blow out" (food *and* beer) at a moderately-priced franchise restaurant; it marked the saying of our goodbyes before I drove my truck-load of books to the heretofore-unglimpsed state of Connecticut. It wasn't the first time that someone has yelled at me in a restaurant, by the way. I don't even think it was the first time someone has yelled at me in a Marie Callender's restaurant. But it was the first time anybody has ever yelled at me, at length and in volume, for disliking a book. Oddly enough, I didn't even hate Toni Morrison's *Beloved* at the time. I just had trouble reading through its middle pages, and seeing what the fuss was all about.

THERE ARE TWO reasons why the title of this essay appealed to me so much that I decided to write an essay to back it up.

First, it strikes me as an almost unspeakable statement in modern culture. In an apparently jaded age, it actually seems to anger and shock people; and, unlike most expressions of relative value, it makes me hesitate before uttering it. Now, let me say that I hate a lot of things, and

8

hating them has rarely gotten me into any trouble, or caused anybody to yell at me in restaurants. I hate, for example, margarine. I hate chemical sweeteners, automatic transmissions, B-format paperbacks, and just about every book Norman Mailer has ever published. I hate that smarmy sitcom "Friends," George W Bush and Al Gore, the CBS Evening News with Dan Rather, Jay Leno (who's going to burn in hell someday, I swear), genetically modified food, rap music, static electricity, Bruce Willis, the Modern Language Association, kiwi fruit, and the Grammys. We all like and dislike different things, love and hate them, but we accept that personal opinion is a free-form, shoot-from-the-hip business, so we try to tolerate one another, and not get too bent out of shape when we like and dislike different things. But hating Toni Morrison's most famous novel seems to bother people in a rather exceptional way, especially when you teach literature (as I do) at University.

There's a second problem with uttering the statement, "I hate Toni Morrison's *Beloved*": it may actually be unhearable. As a statement of personal opinion, preference, idiosyncrasy, taste, what have you, I don't feel people hear this statement in itself, since all sorts of cultural, social and historical meaning gets tangled up with it. To take an obvious example, an Anglo-Irish non-denominational suburban guy such as myself will be "heard" in a variety of ways that he might never wish to be heard; and, whether he likes it or not, all sorts of assumptions might be inferred about his opinions regarding history, race, politics, power and so forth. Or, to dispense with the issue of race altogether (something that's not easy to do when discussing *Beloved*), I might even be accused of writerly bad faith. I mean, we writers are an envious lot, and here I am hating a book which has succeeded spectacularly in ways that none of mine ever have or, I can admit it now, ever will–such as winning the Nobel prize, appearing on Oprah, and selling a gazillion copies.

Finally, the quote-issue-unquote of gender can't be overlooked; certainly not by myself since the night my friend yelled at me. At the time, I was told that my inability to appreciate (to the fullest possible extent) Toni Morrison's *Beloved* was the result of my genetic failures as a socio-sexual entity. The argument ran, as I recall, thus:

> as a man I was threatened by the success of a woman novelist, being essentially incapable of embracing her radically new perspective on history which could only be generated by all-embracing female heterogeneity; in fact, by disliking Morrison, I was validating many opinions that my female colleagues already held about me and the fact that I had completed my Ph.D so quickly in a manifestly sexist English Department, since at least one member of my committee was a known sexist who had reputedly engaged in a long-standing affair with a fellow graduate student . . .

And so forth. It really did continue for a while, dredging up a lot of unspoken emotions. Some of them surprised me; others didn't. I won't belabor this conversation, or the way my statement was "heard" by an individual whom I liked, respected, and continue to be friends with. But I want to place this anecdotal moment in the context of contemporary academic scholarship, since I don't consider it arbitrary or inconsequential. In many ways, it strikes me as surprisingly representative of contemporary scholarly thought.

To put it simply, there are many issues of importance raised by the ways my statement ("I hate Toni Morrison's *Beloved*") can be heard, or misheard, by intelligent individuals. Sex, race, the history of slavery, the responsibilities of men and women for their collective history, the canonization of texts, the subversion of existing canons–all these issues should be addressed, and often are, when we talk about books in University. And we would be remiss if we didn't talk about them, or consider the ways in which they shape our classes, our thinking, and our curriculums.

But this doesn't get me past my two immediate concerns as a reader and a writer:

1) I have trouble saying that I hate Toni Morrison's *Beloved*, mainly because I don't want people to think I am either a racist or a sexist, and

2) people have trouble hearing what I think I'm saying

As a teacher of so-called Literature, where does that leave me when I try to teach *Beloved*? If neither I, nor my students, can express a simple statement of opinion or conviction, where does that leave us when called upon to explore more difficult issues? And where does it leave the common reader who picks up books and puts them down again according to the many multifaceted, and deeply-idiosyncratic reasons we all pick up books and put them down again?

As academics, can we even begin to discuss what it means to read, enjoy, and dislike books?

LET ME CONTINUE by saying that we now have two subjects under discussion. On the one hand, there is the specific book that I hold in my possession. A blue jacketed 38th printing Plume paperback that I purchased across the street from the University of Connecticut at the Paperback Trader. This is a limited, identifiable object that I will return to in a little while. On the other hand, there is this, I don't know what to call it exactly, this illimitable presence, this "landmark of contemporary literature," this vast region of awareness and light and spiritual transmogrification which stands over us in judgment, a manifest recognition which can only be called

Toni Morrison's *Beloved*

I've set these words off in 20-point boldface type, which doesn't do justice to the way I see them projected on the screen of our collective cultural imagination. There, they flicker above and behind all our heads, just out of vision, emitting a vibratory thrum, like a neon sign. You can feel it in the air before you glimpse it. To my mind, 20-point type doesn't do these words justice. 30-point type, perhaps. 40-point. But then I wouldn't have any space left over for writing this essay. There would just be page after page of

Toni Morrison's
Beloved

Which might be a little hard to take.

Now maybe it's my imagination, but whenever I hear those words spoken, 20-point or 40-point or whatever, they are accompanied by a little sigh, a half-sensible expiration. The speaker places a hand on his or her chest, as if a little woozy in admiration. They aren't just speaking the name of a book, you see; they are speaking their own puny inarticulacy in the face of this, this thing called

Toni Morrison's *Beloved*

A silence falls over us in our divided spaces.
I mean, what else can you say?
It's up there, behind me now, looking down as I type

these words. This vast pulsing network of affirmation, filled with inexpressible superlatives. Finest. Greatest. Most Important. Unparalleled. Highest magnitude.

You have to love it or.

Or.

I would like to get to this "or" in a moment.

ACCORDING TO THE MLA guide, the past ten years have seen the publication of more than five hundred articles in respectably vetted journals on the subject of

Toni Morrison's *Beloved*

And almost every one of them is laudatory in the extreme. Occasionally you might find an article which appears value-neutral–examining image-clusters or ideological configurations or whatever–but for the most part these articles never make a negative or qualifying statement about *Beloved*; and they almost always refer to it as a masterpiece, or one of the 20th century's greatest novels, or something along those lines.

At my University library, for example, one and a half shelves are devoted to Toni Morrison, and most of them contain the word *Beloved* in their title, or in one of their chapter titles. And each year, many more books on the subject are published, along with at least two or three introductory texts for beginning students, since *Beloved* is already a significant topic on everything from the SATs to your next Master's exam. Now the liberal academy often likes to congratulate itself for being "open-minded" on the subject of books and ideas; our systems of tenure and advancement are built upon the unexamined assumption that it is not what you say that counts, but how responsibly you say it. But if you would like to investigate just how tolerant the academy really is to disagreement within its ranks, you might like to read one of these introductory-surveys to Toni Morrison's *Beloved*.

Take, as a purely arbitrary example (it's on top of the stack of books I've been assembling in my office) the Ikon Critical Guide, edited by Carl Plasa. This survey of critical essays and topics contains interviews with Morrison, framing comments by the editor, and a fairly standard critical bibliography. Subtitled "the student guide to secondary sources," it is designed to teach students how to compare and analyze arguments, then extrapolate new arguments of their own. And like most books teaching you how to do something, it teaches you how not to do some things as well. What it teaches you not to do is pretty frightening.

In his Introduction, Plasa reminds us of the existing approbation: that Morrison is a "superstar," and "the American and African American (woman) writer to reckon with." And that ever since *Beloved*'s publication, almost every critic and reviewer has been "fully in step" with the "general acclaim"–the only notable exception being an article in *The New Republic* by "the right-wing commentator, Stanley Crouch." As Plasa goes on to explain (just so you know what to think about Crouch's review when you get to it, sixteen pages later):

> The extract from Crouch, by contrast, is a denunciation of *Beloved*/Morrison, as vehement as it is both scurrilous and wrong-headed. Running thoroughly counter to the overwhelmingly positive critical reaction to *Beloved*, it is included here less in the interests of some spurious critical balance than as an illustration of just how highly charged debates about Morrison's work can sometimes be.

"Highly charged," indeed. I guess it's a good thing that even-handed critics like Plasa are around to help the cooler heads prevail; perhaps this is why he prefaces Crouch's review with a comment by Nancy Petersen, which accuses Crouch of "capitalizing on the desire of white readers to consume black women's tales of being abused by black men." (I'm sorry, but I have no idea what that means.) Plasa then takes every opportunity to misread or selectively quote from Crouch in order to make some pretty damning statements. At one point, he claims that Crouch, insensitive to the brutality of slavery, refers to the Middle Passage as little more than a "trip across the Atlantic." This is an inaccurate and misleading statement. Crouch doesn't appear to suggest anything of the sort–though he does argue that Morrison misreads historical events in order to validate modern presumptions, especially feminist ones.

I must confess that I don't know much about Stanley Crouch. I saw him interviewed recently on PBS, so I know he's black; he writes for the *New Republic*, a weekly news and commentary magazine out of D.C. which I have no interest in reading; and he clearly knows how to get up people's noses. His work may well reflect some serious cultural and political biases; but the same could be said of Plasa and his colleagues, pumping away on their critical Stairmasters. Finally, though, I wouldn't call Crouch's review of *Beloved* any more "wrong-headed" or irresponsible than any of those reprinted by Plasa; at least he writes more clearly than they do, and raises some interesting and contentious points–the job, I believe, of any critic or, for that matter, any teacher.

His points may not be agreeable to those who like or admire *Beloved*, but they deserve fair-minded consideration and reply. They don't, however, get them.

IN SUMMARY, HERE are some of the things a young student might learn from the first twenty or thirty pages of Plasa's book, thus equipping him or her for a noble, high-flying career in literary scholarship:

1) some white male and female academics consider themselves incapable of saying anything about *Beloved*–though this doesn't render them incapable of asserting that Toni Morrison represents "a major figure of our national literature"

2) everybody who loves *Beloved* is "fully in step" with the vast mass of scholarship being produced today

3) anybody who disagrees with points 1) or 2) above is probably "scurrilous," and "wrong headed", and may well be pandering to white readers who like to see black women abused by black men.

That's quite a lesson. Even if you do know what it means.

AT THIS POINT, I should make it clear that I'm not interested in discussing contemporary theories of race and gender, or what's called political correctness, or canonization, or even in "deconstructing" the ethno-European aesthetic. What I want to discuss is the overpowering sense I get, walking down the corridors of any literature department in any university anywhere in the world, that my relationship to an individual book (in this case, my 38th printing B-format paperback of *Beloved*) is overseen, and in some sense monitored, by this huge presence called

Toni Morrison's *Beloved*

A presence elevated above and behind us all, in a region that we can't quite see. A presence enforced, glamorized, and idolized by books like the one edited by Plasa, books which depict canonical texts (even while denigrating the process of canonization) as somehow irrefutable, momentous, and a lot more important than we are.

And I have to say that I hate that. I really, really hate

Toni Morrison's *Beloved*

I hate the smugness of it. I hate the sanctimony. I hate the unquestioning sense of itself. And I hate everything about it that takes the individual book out of the individual reader's hand. This hateable thing clearly isn't limited to *Beloved*, by the way. In some ways, I might have entitled this essay, say, why I hate

Herman Melville's *Moby Dick*

a book that I have enjoyed hating with genuine conviction over the years. I studied American Literature in grad school, and wrote my dissertation (and a subsequent book) on it, and while I've always liked the man Melville appears to have been, and many passages of *Moby Dick* are undeniably angry and beautiful and unique, I've always considered it a big fat drag to read from beginning to end. I'll concede that you can learn all sorts of things about American culture from it; it can be fun to teach, and to be taught; and Melville had a lot of interesting observations about consumer culture, racism, and those institutions of slavery that he saw around him as a sailor, a writer, and a clerk. But there are still many books I'd rather take on my next plane trip; it contains far too many descriptions of harpoons; and out of all the dozens of articles and books I've read on the subject of *Moby Dick*, none of them have more accurately defined my feelings for it than this statement from one of my best (and first) students: "It's just too long."

Because that statement comes to my mind every time I see, or discuss, or consider discussing Melville's *Moby Dick*. Not a lot of blather about landmarks of literature cultural hegemony deconstructing the western metaphysic blah blah but just the simple fact of it in your hand, and the daily task of reading it.

Moby Dick is simply "too long."

Put that in your dissertation and smoke it.

OR PERHAPS I could have talked about why I hate

Gunter Grass's *The Tin Drum*

which I simply never got through, or

Rushdie's *Midnight's Children*

which, sure, it's probably a very intelligent book and has lots to say about post-colonial rhetoric and so on, but Rushdie has a wooden ear and his sentences are, I'm afraid, just too angular and klunky. And while we're at it, we could add Pynchon's *Gravity's Rainbow* to the list, or anything by William Burroughs or Kerouac (what a couple of boozy old phonies) and maybe it's already time to hate Jonathan Franzen's *The Corrections*, which I can hate without having read it since everybody seems to love it without having read it simply, as I understand, because the book was selected by Oprah for her annoying book club, and then the ham-fisted author made some impolitic statements which he very hastily retracted. (I mean, there are lots of reasons for loving a book–but really!) All these books that I've tried to read, or could only bring myself to read by virtue of an unwritten contract with the disciplinary institution that pays my salary. Books that are bigger than I am, and bigger than my students, staring down at us from behind, and inviting us to share our opinions just so long as we don't say anything "scurrilous" such as, say, that we don't like them.

All these books, and all these opinions about books, which have nothing to do with anything that goes on in my mind when I read books. And that's the part that puzzles me, and makes me angry.

Why is it that I hate so many of the books I'm supposed to love? And what makes me so mad at them?

BEFORE I TRY to answer those last two questions, I'd like to return to the subject of this specific book, the paperback, remember. 38th printing, blue cover, purchased second-hand for $2 from the Paperback Trader in the late Spring of 1999. It features an author photo of an attractive, middle-aged woman, along with some pretty impressive jacket copy, most notably:

Winner of
THE NOBEL PRIZE
in
Literature

and a highly-placed quote from the important American reviewer, John Leonard, who says, "I can't imagine American literature without it."

Now I don't know about you, but I can imagine American literature without *Moby Dick*, so I'd have to say that John Leonard is pretty impressed. *Beloved* hasn't simply enlightened him or given him pleasure: it has redefined the parameters of his world.

Good going, *Beloved*.

When I hold this particular copy of this particular book in my hand, I do not feel alone; nor do I feel like a free individual with his own thoughts and opinions. The presence of

Toni Morrison's *Beloved*

looms oppressively, its bristly tentacles and veiny suction devices wrapped invisibly around me, coated with a treacly substance. It entangles my limbs and thoughts, attaching itself to my nerves and vertebrae and belly, like one of those pod-spiders in *The Matrix*. In order to read this book, clearly and simply, as one person reads any book in the privacy of his own room or head, I require something I don't normally bring to a reading experience. I require an act of will; and a monumental act of forgetting. I must uproot all the snake-like wiring and suction creatures. I must find my own way in the book, word after word and page after page. And frankly, I don't know how well I can do that. I don't know how well I can let this book speak for itself, outside that sanctimonious reverberating thrum of

Toni Morrison's *Beloved*

So I will do my best to think clearly about what I've read. And come to think of it, the conclusions I've reached are probably a lot more radical than saying I hate it, or it's bad, or it shouldn't be read. My final conclusions would probably go a little like this:

It starts off really well; the central character of Sethe, and the haunting of her family, is strange and surprising and beautifully written; but the book never recovers from the arrival of the mysterious ghost-girl. I lose sight of Sethe; and the succubus doesn't work for me at all–some of the passages told through her eyes strike me as sentimental and slightly phony, like bad beat poetry. Finally, I don't like it when the town's wise women come along at the end to sort things out; I'm always annoyed by books where the women turn out to be so much more noble and capable than the stupid men, since it's the long-reigning trope of just about every TV commercial I've ever seen since I was three years old. ("Oh, honey, stop fiddling with that drain. Just pick up the phone and call Roto-Rooter!")

I've been in academia long enough to know that all my objections to *Beloved* can be explained away by critical methodology–theories of alterity and the *mise en abyme* and so forth. ("You're supposed to feel lost when the succubus appears–because you're experiencing Sethe's self-estrangement.") I'm sure I suffer from my fair share of cultural misconceptions; I'm not as smart as I should be; and the fact I don't get the point of *Beloved* probably is precisely its point. But I can also say that none of these theories have anything to do with the way I read books. Nor do they explain the pleasures I experience when reading a book that I enjoy, or the annoyance I feel when I'm reading a book that I don't.

NOW I'VE PROBABLY done an imperfect job of explaining why I hate

Toni Morrison's *Beloved*

and why I find the individual act of reading my particular copy pretty hard going. But I wanted to conclude by describing my own history with books, and why I love some of them, and why I hate others. I want to do this because after years of teaching literature, studying it, and reviewing it for various international newspapers and magazines, my elemental feelings about books seem to have gotten lost along the way. And the act of remembering those feelings is an important part of both reading and teaching. Far more important, to my mind, than anything I ever learned from a critical text, or in a classroom.

LIKE MANY PEOPLE who enjoy books, I have fond memories of being read to as a child. It is strange to think that while my parents did many things for me when I was growing up—fed and clothed and housed me—that I remember evening bedtime stories with a special gratitude. In my early years, before my younger brother was born, my parents would guide me through large picture books—I especially enjoyed the ones filled with photographs of lions and tigers and zebras. Later, we read books with fewer pictures and more words; books which I didn't understand, sometimes, and didn't need to. There was something about the ritual warmth of reading that mattered more than what the words conveyed. Cuddling up around the book with my brother and one of my parents and listening to that night's chapter of *Call of the Wild*, say, or *Alice in Wonderland*; asking questions about what would happen next ("I don't know, we'll have to wait until tomorrow to find out, won't we?") And, finally, going to bed with these weird visions of other worlds in my head. I might imagine myself and my brother riding bobsleds across the frozen steppes, hurrying to save poor Buck from his lapse into savagery; or sitting down to tea with the Mad Hatter; or helping Black Beauty return to her long lost master. They weren't better than me, these books. They were inseparable from my imagination. And they didn't speak at my mind. They conversed with it.

Eventually, I learned to read books for myself. I preferred stories about traveling to faraway countries and planets, and commonly the word "Voyage" figured in the titles, such as *A Voyage to the Mushroom Planet*, or *The Voyages of Doctor Doolittle*. I was also intrigued by stories about boys who built things in their basements—zoos, printing presses, secret laboratories—and achieved worldwide renown. Sherlock Holmes figured prominently on my bookshelf. I read everything I could find about Sherlock Holmes.

About the same time that I was reading books to find

out what was in them, I was already growing intrigued by the mass, volume and variety of all the books I couldn't read. Both of my parents had been to college, and their old textbooks were assembled in a long, waist-high wooden bookshelf that divided the living room from the hallway in our suburban tract-home in San Luis Obispo, California. If I lay down in the hallway, hidden away from my parents in the smack dab middle of the house, I found myself in this "secret place" of books. They included quite a few dog-eared and spine-warped bestsellers, such as the James Bond novels my Dad was always reading, and about which he seemed vaguely embarrassed. ("They're kind of like grown-up comic-books," he used to say.) Then there were my mother's nursing textbooks, which featured glossy schemata of bowels and reproductive organs and brains and lymphatic tissue. And finally, there were the "adult story books." Most of these were in Modern Library editions, without even jackets anymore to illustrate what they were about. There were only the uniform dark gray spines, names of authors and titles embossed in flaking gilt, and the figure of a tiny ankle-winged Hermes, messenger of the Gods, weirdly poised like a ballet dancer. These books contained no pictures to show me what was going on in them, so I had to figure them out for myself.

I still remember the titles of these books as vividly as anything I have ever read. There was *Of Human Bondage*, of course. I had no trouble at all imagining what that was about. Some brave man, captured by Indians, lay trussed up in a closet for 837 pages until he triumphed, broke free, and saved his family from being burned at the stake. Then there was *War and Peace* (which couldn't be half bad), and *Native Son* (young Navaho seeks freedom on the plains), and finally *Pride and Prejudice*, which, somewhere on the periphery of my suburb-locked understanding, seemed to invoke all these news reports I had been hearing about long hot summers and bussing in the south.

I remember loving *Moby Dick* before I read it. What's

not to love when you're five years old? This one-legged Captain driving his crew to sail the seven seas in search of a gigantic white whale? What a great book not to read. I even loved the movie when I was little (it was on par with *The Amazing Colossal Man*, though it didn't give me so many nightmares), and I went on to purchase the Classics Illustrated edition at the local Rexall drug store. I endlessly read and re-read this Classics Illustrated edition, carrying it around scrunched up in my back pocket until it resembled the head of a mop. In fact, I read it so often and so intensely that, many years later as an undergraduate at UCLA, I got away without reading the actual book on at least two exams. I have many friends who love Melville, and I hope that the day arrives when I can say I like Melville as much as I loved that Classics Illustrated comic book. In my most subjective universe, that would be saying something.

Then there was *The Brothers Karamazov*, another one of those titles that jumped out at me when I was five years old. I had a brother three years younger than myself, and we were very close, so I figured it had something to do with us, and the games we played together. My mother aroused my interest even further by informing me that it concerned a murder ("Great!") and finding out who did it ("Even better!") and that one of the four brothers who might have committed the murder was an atheist who didn't believe in God.

Wow, I thought. And, for that matter, still do.

For me, Dostoevsky has always been one of those rare writers who lives up to the hype.

I REMEMBER THIS space on the hall floor, surrounded by books I couldn't quite read, with great fondness. Those books were far from objects of worship. I played with them. I stacked them in interesting configurations—pyramids and rectangles and obelisks. And I imagined what might happen if the characters they contained were to wander out of their books and move into one another's territories. Would Ellison's *Invisible Man* be a match for the *Invisible Man* of H.G. Wells? Would Mailer's naked soldiers perform bizarre and unconscionable acts with Samuel Butler's flesh-bound travelers–very likely in a hot bath before bedtime? I played with these books, and never felt I had any responsibility to them. And I was committed to reading them someday because I wanted to know what was in them. If I didn't like what was in them, I could put them aside and read something else. Whenever I think about books, or the act of reading, with pleasure and affection, I always think about this time I spent alone on the floor with those books I couldn't yet read. I recall it as the best possible relationship with books I have ever known.

SOMETHING HAS HAPPENED to the reading of books in my lifetime. I don't want to sound like one of those cranky old men who says everything was better in my day, because I don't think it was. But the worst aspects of book-reading have slowly taken the place of the better ones; and when it comes to academic writing on the subject of literature, it doesn't take a stylistic genius to recognize that the prose has grown dense, convoluted, and unreadable. Academics seem to select a few books each year as worthy of consideration without having read anything else. Then they congratulate one another for liking the same books, before picking petty arguments about which end of the book should be cracked first. Which book is more reactionary than the other two? Which undermines gender stereotypes more effectively, or unravels the always-unraveling thread of language? At the end of the day, you don't feel anybody is talking about books at all. They're talking about themselves, and the disciplinary institution called, for want of a better term, literary culture. They're talking about their boring jobs.

When I think about all those huge indigestible books up there behind us, I think about the statues on Easter

Island that were erected by people we don't know much about. Statues bigger than us, more frightening, and more real than we're supposed to be, and I think that I can live with the statues somebody erected a few hundred thousand years ago. But I can't bear to watch my colleagues, and my students, and myself, straining in concert to erect more of them. I don't want to see any more statues raised on Easter Island, and the real reason I hate Toni Morrison's *Beloved* is that, whatever its merits, it is the statue I have watched being raised in my lifetime.

Books are about a lot of things. Race, gender, the Napoleonic Wars, sex, death, food, social norms, social outcasts, social incasts, fantasy, fact, dreams, sadness, loneliness, elation, injustice, class, the Mason-Dixon line, language, stupidity, co-habitation and rage. But ultimately, they are about the process of reading them; they are about the things their author has known and seen and imagined long enough to write them down.

At the risk of sounding corny or sentimental, I would like to propose a very ad hoc definition of books. I'd like to suggest that they are not any better than us, nor do they have much to teach us. Books are simply a place where we try to imagine everything that is best and worst in us. As such, it is an always-dangerous place, and always unsettling. And it never congratulates us for what we're already thinking. At its best, it leads us into thinking about people and places and ideas different from ourselves. We don't need to like the writers behind the books we enjoy reading, because they are usually just people. But we do owe them the not-inconsiderable gift of reading them as carefully as we can.

When I first thought up the title of this essay, I felt uncertain and defensive about it. But in the course of writing it, I have come to conclude that I don't mind hearing anybody say they hate or love any book, or any writer. To hear people disagreeing about books, hating and loving them, doesn't make some of those people good people, and other ones bad people. It doesn't sound like a bunch of "right wing" people arguing with a bunch of "fully in step" ones. It just sounds like the noisy contentious clash and accord of people reading. The most terrible statement you can utter is not "I hate X" or "I love Y." The most terrible thing you can say, especially to your students, is: "You must hate X." Or: "You must love Y."

Our relationships with books are not a set of decisions handed down to us. They are a series of decisions we make every day of our lives. And at the risk of sounding sentimental, I suggest these decisions should not be made while looking over our shoulders at the looming monstrosities of our critical present. Rather they are decisions we should make together, each of us alone in our imperfect heads, continually glancing at one another for confirmation, elucidation, and contradiction, with the books stacked up around us, and lying on the floor.

The Denver Quarterly – 2004

Hating Beloved–the Post-Game Summary

IN 2001, SOMEBODY called me on the phone six months before I was scheduled to speak in Berlin and requested the title of my lecture. They were paying good money, so I felt I should try something new–a "personal essay."

My desk at UCONN was covered with these terrible "How to Teach *Beloved*" textbooks I'd been picking up at used bookstores because, frankly, I had no idea how to teach *Beloved*. And I was getting frustrated. So I said, "I'd like to write about why I hate Toni Morrison's *Beloved*." The Berliners printed up lots of flyers, ran ads in newspapers, and six months later, I had cornered myself into writing this essay.

After the lecture, a young blondish Paul Verhoeven-looking Austrian man stood up and said, sounding a lot like Governor Arnold, that he was disappointed I hadn't really blasted Toni Morrison, and that I should have kept my promise. Then he walked out.

I turned the lecture into a prose-essay the next year, when I taught a graduate seminar at UCONN entitled, "Literature and Crap: What We Like and What We're Supposed To." For two years, I sent the essay around to dozens of journals and periodicals, all of whom rejected it on one of two grounds:

1) they "didn't get it"

2) they agreed that they didn't like the book either, and agreed with most of the things I said, but they

"just couldn't" publish it

The essay was eventually accepted by a young(er than me) critic and short story writer named Paul Maliszewski, who was guest-editing *The Denver Quarterly*. Paul accepted the essay, and subjected it to his version of close-editing– which was excruciating, never-ending, and, more often than not, really helpful. Shortly after the essay was published, Paul wrote me an e-mail which said something like: "Oh, and there's this awkward phrase on page seventeen we still need to look at." It was the only e-mail from Paul to which I never replied.

I have been snubbed several times since the essay appeared by people who wanted me to know it. At one dinner party, a colleague and his partner picked up their plates and left the room when I suggested that Charles Johnson (a good novelist and short story writer I have never met) had every right to say that he didn't like *Beloved* (I don't know if he did say that, by the way, but that's what somebody had reported). And still, every so often, I will meet an academic who will say to me, "*Beloved* is a very, very important book to me." They say it completely out of the blue. Then they drop the subject and walk away.

The essay was never reprinted or made available on the Internet. So I was glad that Eric and Eliza agreed to make it available at Two Dollar Radio, where we are all encouraged to freely love and hate books as we see fit. Even our own.

After the essay appeared in print in 2004, I received a few clandestine nudges and winks from people who told me they liked the essay, but that was all. Then, a few months ago, somebody sent me Wikipedia's entry on *The Denver Quarterly*, which described one of *DQ*'s high points as the "published to acclaim" Morrison essay. (And I didn't write the entry, I swear.)

I sent the entry to Paul Maliszsewski, who promised me he hadn't written it either. Then he suggested that "published to acclaim" was probably a cliché, so we should cut it.

"Please don't," I replied.

Two Dollar Radio Blog – 2010

Paradise of the Damned: California Writers

SERIOUS WRITERS AREN'T supposed to live in California. They aren't supposed to frolic on white beaches, or drive convertibles down PCH, or attend script conferences with Tic-Tac-popping studio executives, where the only issue in dispute is how much to be paid, and how soon. Rather, serious writers are supposed to be true to their vision, attend Ivy League/Oxbridge universities, happily publish books that don't sell, and live in derelict bed-sits close to their publishers in New York, London, and Paris. In other words, they are expected to dream more conventional dreams than California. Otherwise, they might appear as vain and materialistic as the critics who applaud them after they're dead.

Living at the sudden-as-a-cliff-edge-finality of westward-yearning Manifest-Destiny, California writers are out of the .loop, and this is part of their charm. Eccentrically-entrepreneurial and poorly-networked, they sop up their messy educations at local libraries and second-hand bookstores (*a la* Steinbeck and Jack London); publish their work through fly-by-night small presses (Bukowski and the various Beats); or assemble their *oeuvres* through the always-underestimated pulp-paperback houses (Philip K. Dick and Jim Thompson). California writers are a motley, distinctly unserious lot. This is because most of them have been knocking around for so long in America's largest state (the State of Mind, natch) that they don't know what they are *supposed* to do.

Which is, of course, what makes them interesting.

"I KNOW YOU'RE mad at me for being a Hollywood whore," John Fante once wrote his New York agent, "but it's fun while it lasts." Which is probably a lot more than can be said about most literary whoredoms—academic, journalistic, or even those eligible for the Booker. Say what you will about California writers, they do what they do with passionate intensity—and they don't mind having a little fun in the sun while they're doing it. And while eccentric self-invention may be their one over-riding characteristic, most of them can be slotted into one of the following four essential categories: the Hard-Boiled, the Spaced Out, the Street-Wise, and the Hippy Dippy.

Most California writers, by the way, won't be bothered by such disparaging terminology, since being disparaged is something they know about.

THE HARD-BOILED School—having succeeded in the only literary terms that matter these days (making money)—is now accepted as capital-L Literature. And not coincidentally, it is a genre which depicts California as an urban *noir* of mean streets, disconnected lives, and random violence where a few firm, good men (carrying guns, of course) try to sort out the demons from the angels—and usually bring their soft-spoken form of vigilante justice to the proceedings just a few minutes too late. From *The Big Sleep* and *The Player* to *Pulp Fiction* and *L.A. Confidential*, the dispassionate lens of *noir* scans California's tacky suburbs to divulge the secret histories of money, property, strange sex and bad faith. In a land where anybody can be whoever they want to be (unless, of course, they change their minds), these novelists don't delve too deeply into the question of who people really are, but rather trace the causal chain of one person knocking into another and another, bang bang bang, in escalating complications until somebody winds up dead. Even Pynchon's great California novels, *Vineland* and *The Crying of Lot 49*, are about revealing conspiracies of meaning which, in the long run, mean nothing at all.

When it comes to being Spaced-Out, nobody has been there and done that like Philip K. Dick. (Though a few religion-builders–L. Ron Hubbard, say, or Annie Besant– definitely gave him a run for his money.) Raised in the Bay Area, Dick was the sort of life-long Californian who wore his belief-systems loosely. And like many of his own characters–in novels as solipsistically-diverse as *Martian Time-Slip*, *The Three Stigmata of Palmer Eldritch* and *Do Androids Dream of Electric-Sheep?*–Dick claimed to have enjoyed both out-of-body experiences, and telepathic communication with interstellar beings. Conventional reality, for Dick, was something people cooked up in order to sell Barbie doll accessories and Mickey Mouse watches, so it is probably no surprise that his always-dissembling virtual worlds have been discovered by the movie business. Hollywood executives likewise seem to believe that reality is something you do to earn a buck–or you don't bother doing it at all.

But while the Hard Boiled and Spaced Out schools are among the most successful manifestations of the West Coast *Weltanschauung*, they aren't necessarily the best. And despite their current cinematic unpopularity, the Street-Wise crew represents California's most substantive literary-elite. Beginning with the socialist and Naturalist novelists– Upton Sinclair (*The Jungle*), Jack London (*Call of the Wild*) and Steinbeck (*In Dubious Battle*)–the Street-Wisers crested into the twentieth century in the guise of John Fante, a transplanted Italo-Coloradoan who published one of the most emblematic Southern-California novel of his generation, *Ask the Dust*, back in 1939. Like many California novels, *Ask the Dust* is semi-autobiographical, and describes an inner-city populated both by those who, in the words of Nathanael West, "had come to California to die," and those who came there to live too well:

> …Dust and old buildings and old people sitting at windows, old people tottering out of doors, old people moving painfully along the dark street. The old folk from Indiana and Iowa and Illinois, from Boston and Kansas City and Des Moines, they sold their homes and their stores, and they came here by train and by automobile to the land of sunshine, to die in the sun, with just enough money to lie until the sun killed them, tore themselves out by the roots in their last days, deserted the smug prosperity of Kansas City and Chicago and Peoria to find a place in the sun. And when they got here they found that other and greater thieves had taken possession, that even the sun belonged to the others; Smith and Jones and Parker, druggist, banker, baker, dust of Chicago and Cincinnati and Cleveland on their shoes, doomed to die in the sun, a few dollars in the bank, enough to subscribe to the Los Angeles Times, enough to keep alive the illusion that this was paradise, that their papier-mâché homes were castles. The uprooted ones, the empty sad folks, the old and the young folks, the folks from back home. These were my countrymen, these were the new Californians. With their bright polo shirts and sunglasses, they were in paradise, they belonged.

For Fante, California was a Paradise that people created for themselves. But a Paradise, nevertheless.

Finally, California's most unfairly disparaged writer could well be Richard Brautigan, who breathed life into the Hippy-Dippy school during the Woodstock-era. By means of a series of funny, episodic and surreal comic novels, such as *A Confederate General From Big Sur* and *Trout Fishing in America*, Brautigan has remained a cult-favorite on college campuses for three decades since his death, but his literary stature has never been writ large.

Ianthe Brautigan's memoir of coming to terms with her father's suicide (Brautigan shot himself in the head at forty-seven) suffers from many *longueurs*, but depicts a genuinely talented and gentle man who wasn't at his best when he started drinking. Brautigan fled rural poverty in the Pacific Northwest, not to mention a brief stint in a Salem mental ward, to become the porkpie-hatted, walrus-mustached and very Whitmanesque poet who adorned his own dust-jackets, usually flanked by a distinctive-looking young woman (just to let it be known he wasn't *that* Whitmanesque). For Brautigan, art was supposed to be, well, here comes that word again–"fun." Sometimes, though, fun had its drawbacks, such as the night Brautigan took his daughter to see Nureyev at the San Francisco Opera House, and was dismayed to learn that none of the performers in this particular ballet were ever going to start talking.

"I'm going to go get a drink," he decided finally.

It was the same bad decision that Brautigan continued making over and over again.

ALONG WITH DAUGHTER Ianthe's memoir, Rebel Inc. is publishing something unusual: a posthumous novel which is actually quite good, one of Brautigan's best, in fact. And while it recounts the last days of a writer who thinks too much about suicide, *An Unfortunate Woman* never ceases to be moving or surprising, and contains some of Brautigan's best work.

In some ways, though, this too-long-delayed posthumous novel reinforces a sad misimpression that California is often the last gasp of dying talents. For while many fine writers certainly died there–Fitzgerald, West and Stevenson, to name a few–they probably would have died even quicker just about anywhere else. And, undoubtedly, they wouldn't have had as much fun doing it, or enjoyed nicer weather.

(London) Times – 2000

Philip K. Dick–a Life out of Joint

IN PHILIP K. Dick's fictional universe, truth is an idea cooked up in order to sell Perky Pat doll accessories and Mickey Mouse watches. Time runs backwards; undercover cops spy on everybody (including themselves); and hard-working men who can't afford package-holidays to Mars purchase memories of those holidays instead. It's a closed continuum of endless strip-malls and fast-food franchise restaurants, offering perpetual freedom of movement but no place anybody wants to go.

In many ways, Dick was the ultimate California-novelist. Self-taught, disdained by New York literary publishers, and something of a crackpot, he tried every drug he could get his hands on, and explored every religion that promised a way out of himself. And whatever he did, he did too much of. He married five times, wrote more than three-dozen novels, and dreamed some pretty weird dreams. At various times in his life he claimed to be the target of FBI covert ops, of John Bircher "attack force" vendettas, and of KGB *Mission: Impossible*-style surveillance techniques. "I took the Minnesota Multiphasic psychological profile test once," Dick confessed in a 1980 interview, "and I tested out as paranoid, cyclothymic, neurotic, schizophrenic… But I also tested out as an incorrigible liar." Like many Californians, Philip K. Dick wasn't always exactly who he claimed to be. Thank goodness.

Even the titles of his novels testify to Dick's peculiar sense of anomie and dislocation: *Time Out of Joint*, *A Maze of Death*, *Eye in the Sky*, *A Handful of Darkness*. The typical Dick protagonist is a lumpy, emotionally-inarticulate Everyman with a muttish name like Ragle Gumm or Stuart McConchie. As an individual he feels authentic; as a social being, he does not. Usually he works with his hands in some menial occupation (TV repairman, jewelry maker or tire-regroover) and wisely distrusts anybody in authority (government officials, television "news clowns", and most of all, cops). Having spent his entire life trying to maintain a fragile grip on reality, that grip begins to loosen. His wife leaves him (if she hasn't already left); he gets fired from his job; impersonal police forces loom; and the world as he knows it vanishes altogether.

Dick's best novels are about people trying to come to terms with their own particular (and peculiar) realities. In the Hugo-award winning *The Man in the High Castle* (1962), Frank Frink lives in an alternate, post World-War II America divided down the middle by triumphant Japanese and German forces. He manufactures fake Civil War memorabilia for people looking for a sense of "historicity", and spends his spare time reading an underground cult-novel that describes yet another alternate world in which America won the war. In a world of perpetually shifting belief-systems, Frank realizes that the worst part about Nazis is that you eventually get used to having them around. Truth doesn't prevail; it shifts.

In *Time Out of Joint* (1959) Ragle Gumm retreats into a fantasy-vision of 1950's America, just so he won't have to face up to the awful future his planet has created for itself. And in Dick's mind-bending pop-masterpiece, *The Three Stigmata of Palmer Eldritch* (1964), expatriates on Mars take drugs in order to live in a Barbie-doll-style paradise of big-breasted women, souped-up sports cars, and really great hi-fi equipment. The lesson of experience, Dick's books argue, is that conspiracies of meaning exist in the world around us–bad governments, arbitrary gods, commercial conglomerates–and they're designed by people as self-interested, unimaginative and fallible as ourselves. "Good grief!" one of Dick's cannier characters exclaims when confronted by a friend's benign faith in computers. "It says IBM right on it! What do you expect it to tell you? The truth?"

ONCE DICK'S CHARACTERS open themselves up to relationships with other people, everything grows unverifiable. And truth (spiritual, personal, and political) becomes a matter of somebody else's point-of-view. In *Flow My Tears, the Policeman Said* (1974) Jason Taverner is a genetically designed TV Variety host in a near future US when his personal reality goes missing. It's not because he has taken drugs and begun redreaming his life, but because someone else has taken drugs and is redreaming him. And in *The Divine Invasion* (1981) Herb Asher (like many Dickian protagonists) lives in an extraterrestrial "hovel" where he works redirecting bad radio and TV programs all over the galaxy. After falling in love with a computer-generated crooner named Linda Fox, he encounters a manipulative all-knowing deity named Yah, who torments him by constantly replaying the all-strings version of *Fiddler on the Roof* in his headset.

Like many Californians, Philip K. Dick wore his belief-systems loosely, and that was part of his charm. Throughout his career he managed to wax enthusiastic about a variety of esoteric philosophies, rarely took any of his own delusions too seriously, and always obeyed Blake's prime directive–if you don't invent your own religion, somebody will invent one for you. Still, there were times when he pushed his personal credibility to the breaking point: he often reported out-of-body experiences; he was a lifelong anti-abortionist who never stuck around long enough to raise any of his own children; and on February

3, 1974 he claimed to make telepathic contact with an interstellar being he dubbed a Vast Active Living Intelligence System. ("On Thursdays and Saturdays I would think it was God, on Tuesdays and Wednesdays I would think it was extraterrestrial, sometimes I would think it was the Soviet Union Academy of Sciences trying out their psychotronic microwave telepathic transmitter.") With customary openness, Dick recounted the experience in his semi-autobiographical novel *VALIS* through the perspective of an eternal skeptic. He was willing to believe these weird things had actually happened; he just didn't want to believe it too hard.

Dick died in 1982 at the age of fifty-three, just as the film-world was starting to catch up with his always-dissembling virtual-worlds. After the cult-success of *Blade Runner* (based on Dick's more aptly-titled 1968 novel, *Do Androids Dream of Electric Sheep?*) and the financial success of *Total Recall* (based on his brilliant 1966 novelette, "We Can Remember It for You Wholesale") Dick's work began generating enormous film-rights advances. As a result, his books are today being enthusiastically republished by the same "literary" publishers who disdained his work in the first place.

Many of Dick's books (especially *Flow My Tears*, *Eldritch*, and *High Castle*, all of which have just been reissued in paperback by Harper-Collins) remain as startling and original today as when they were first published. Others are so clumsily composed and shoddily constructed as to be virtually unreadable. Dick may not have been a great "literary writer" (whatever that means) but like the recently rediscovered thriller-novelists Jim Thompson and Peter Rabe, he was undoubtedly a great writer of commercial paperback fiction, pushing the limits of his preferred genre to the breaking point over a series of books that are truly *sui generis* and disturbing. And even in terms of contemporary mainstream fiction, nobody has written more successfully than Philip K. Dick about extraordinary states of mind. Perhaps because so many of them were his own.

(London) Observer – 1996

Letter from London

I MOVED TO Europe twenty-five years ago to get away from California. And now I think almost constantly about moving back. Go figure.

This is not because I have ever stopped loving London, the first city in the world that made me feel at home. It's more that I have lived here so long that I can now hate it with all the calm conviction of a native. When I "whinge" about the crowded streets, the corrupt middle-class professional culture, the smarmy government, or the bad sandwiches (yes, you can still find them), I like to think that I don't quite sound like an Ugly American. I like to think that I sound like an Ugly Brit.

Not that this makes me very palatable to the English. But then, let's face it–nobody's very palatable to the English. Which is probably why I get along with them so well.

Unlike Californians, the English keep themselves to themselves. They don't hastily tumble across whatever social or interpersonal boundaries stand in their way, flinging open doors and cupboards, sniffing behind curtains and settees. What's more, they don't smear you with their messy interiority, confessing their deepest dreams and aspirations at the drop of a hat. Like puppies (and I have to confess there's a lot of this puppyishness in my nature as well), Californians are too confident in their enthusiasms. Then, when the world surprises them with something unpleasant, they don't take time to understand it. They just bite.

In California, you can find yourself talking to people for hours about who they *really* are, and how they *really* feel, and how their sense of cosmic self-hood often conflicts too much with their spiritual values and so forth, but you never have any idea what they're talking about. Once it gets out of the cage, this inner life of Westerners just multiplies exponentially, like that invading space creature in The Blob.

WHEN I DECIDED to make London my home in the mid-eighties, it was still very deeply English, both for good and bad.

On the debit side: there were few decent moderately-priced restaurants; you couldn't buy Ben and Jerry's ice-cream anywhere; and on bank-holiday weekends, almost every shop closed for two or three days, I'm not kidding. You couldn't buy a pint of milk unless you took a double-decker bus from one end of the city to another, and wiped the dust off the last UHT-impregnated long-lasting waxy-cardboard container of milk in back of a cluttered newsagent shop. For many years, I lived in a tiny converted studio flat that I purchased (at the bloated end of one of London's mega-perilous housing bubbles) not far from the now-infamous Finsbury Park Mosque. This was a largely West-Indian neighborhood, and about three or four doors down from the local Tesco you could find cow-heads hanging outside shops on hooks (if, that is, you were looking for them). I remember when the first American-style 7-11 opened over the hill in Crouch End, back before the neighborhood was over-run by movie actors and rock producers. At that time, you could still find people living in the area who did something useful–carpenters, plumbers and so forth–and when I'd trek over Crouch Hill in the middle of the night to this bright and spangly "convenience store," it felt like journeying to Shangri-La. There I'd run into guys who'd recently fixed my central heating or rerouted my fuse box, and we would marvel at our sudden collective ability to buy things like light bulbs and donuts at three o'clock in the morning, even on a Bank Holiday weekend. But then the new shopping laws came along, and 7-11 disappeared, replaced by more and more various late night and weekend outlets. Today, there's a 24-hour Tesco around the corner from my home in Russell Square, which is constantly packed by jet-lagged American college kids indulging their Krispy-Kreme habits. Sure, it's convenient, but it's not the same as Crouch End at three in the morning. At that time, being able to buy something late night in London was like keeping a beautiful secret. Well-lit, unguarded, and pristine.

There were a lot of things I loved about British London in the mid-eighties, even what is often derogatorily referred to as "English cooking." Such as the British fry-up at a local "caff," which is, to my mind, one of Britain's least-recognized culinary innovations. When Brits go fatty, they go *really* fatty, and I can't tell you how pleased I was to order my first "English breakfast" and be served both a pair of deep-fried British sausages (the best sausages in the world, to my mind) and bacon and eggs and thin-cut deep-fried chips, and even, I swear to god, a thick lardy slice of what they call "fried bread," which is definitely the least nutritious (and most satisfying) way of serving bread in the history of, well, bread. Then to see this heart-stopping fat-fest dripping in really runny baked beans and buttery mushrooms, with a large cup of greasy-looking tea on the side–my mouth waters just thinking about it. It's still my favorite breakfast in the entire world. Also, I don't know why this is true, but if you decide to seek out one of these very anti-Surgeon-General-type breakfasts on your next trip to the Isles, I have one decent piece of advice (and most of my advice, by the way, sucks): the crummier the caff looks, the better the breakfast. I don't know why that is, but it definitely *is*.

THEN, OF COURSE, there's British ale, which is the best beer I've ever known. I actually sip the stuff a bit like wine, which makes me look like a dilettante when I'm sitting with my book in the back of the dullest, quietest pub I can find. Another interesting thing I've learned is that British ale must be drunk out of pint-sized glasses. This doesn't mean you can't order a half pint at a time, but it simply must be poured into a well-toned pint-sized glass. It has something to do with how the fragrance is spun off by the large blobby mouth of the glass. Believe me, I know what I'm talking about. If you drink good British ale out of a half-pint glass, you'll be bitterly disappointed.

Oh, and now that I think about it, I've never actually enjoyed a pint of ale with a British fry-up breakfast. But I've seen it done. And perhaps I will enjoy this experience one day before I die.

ANOTHER THING I loved about London from the start—and this hasn't changed at all—is it's belligerent unchangeable eternal sense of rampant disorder and barely-controlled chaos. It's a city that doesn't make any sense, either on a map, or in the American conception of things like neighborhoods or city blocks; and it continually spills off in oblique tangents and odd little brick byways and surprisingly-off-kilter flights of stairs, like some mammothly-conceived drawing by M. C. Escher. In California, I never felt I belonged amongst the wide-open flux of highway-strewn and telephone-line-knitted spaces. But in London, you are instantly grounded by a massy conjunction of architecture and time. History resounds everywhere, but never makes you feel confined. The only American equivalent would be a place like Los Angeles, with its vast motley of overgrown and discontinuous suburbs. But London has, and always will have, one thing LA never did. Walkable vistas. And in every direction.

London is still an awful place for drivers; I've never even entertained the thought of buying a car here. Thickly intertwined by weird one-way serpentine thoroughfares and insane roundabouts and interlocking bike-paths and concrete-barricaded road-works, London is a huge confusion of public and private spaces. In fact, there are still surprisingly large swathes of London that are actually owned by ridiculous things like earls and dukes and such, who rent out their inherited estates to the American universities and foreign banks, much like their multiply-great grand-daddies did many centuries ago. Meanwhile, amidst these old ancestral demesnes, London's rampant capitalists (and London must be the most fiercely-capitalistic city on earth) have divvied up, subsumed and over-reached every possible loophole in the law–and in spatial harmony–to build radically conflicting intersections of private homes and garden-squares and office blocks and market-stalls. If you ever decide to buy a home in London (and I don't recommend that you do), you will quickly encounter some of these weird class histories and bowdlerized notions of ownership I'm talking about. For example, the flat you want to "lease" for two hundred and fifty years turns out to be owned by the Duke of Velour, or the Earl of Somesuch, but the wobbly paving stones out front are owned by a long-bankrupted squatter who disappeared during the Blitz, and the backyard tree–the roots of which have invaded your downstairs toilet–isn't owned by anybody, so nobody can do anything about it. You never really buy property in London; you only conspire with the long mess of history to borrow it for a while. This is probably why, halfway through every property negotiation, your fleet of lawyers and estate agents and surveyors and the seller's fleet of same collectively agree to disregard at least half of the irresolvable problems they've discovered in the multiply-amended deeds and moldy blueprints recently unearthed at City Hall. Otherwise, nobody could buy anything in this town.

So some dead Earl's tree will always be in deep conflict

with some poor slob's plumbing, that's just the way it is. At least until another slob (or another tree) moves in to take their place. "Get used to it!"–that's the British motto. Which is probably why Brits and Yanks have so much trouble seeing eye-to-eye, since the American motto, as we all know, is: "Fix it. Or knock it down."

ABOUT EIGHT YEARS ago I moved to what I still consider the best part of London, a slice of San Pancras and Bloomsbury that was pretty clearly-demarcated by the bombs of 6/6. One of those bombs erupted deep in the Piccadilly line tunnel that runs underneath my building— where I hear the trains starting up every morning from my bedroom. This rush of underground trains is one of those satisfying sensory impressions that always reassures me I'm home after a long trip abroad, much like the outdoor frying of sausages and onions at Camden market, or the cordite and pigeony ambience of Victoria Station. Another bomb, the one that wrecked the bus at Tavistock Square, went off outside my bank on Southampton Row, and just across the street from Tavistock Square, where my son, his noisy friends and I use to play squirt gun wars among the well-tended flowerbeds and antiwar monuments–a flower-and-garland-bestrewn statue of Gandhi, a tree planted in memory of the victims of Hiroshima, and a large obsidian stone honoring conscientious objectors.

It use to be that many sections of London were noted for their "villagey" atmospheres–the family vendors and outdoor markets and local oddballs–but most of these distinctly-flavorful neighborhoods have been eroded by yuppification, name-brand coffee logos, and tourists. My neighborhood, on the other hand, has retained much of its original flavor over the past three decades by doing what Britain seems to do best: throwing its hands up in the air and letting everybody in. All day and night, fleets of tourists escort their castor-squeaking luggage up and down the sidewalks, or sit out in garden squares with their packaged sandwiches and Meal Deals from the local Boots. Sometimes entire classrooms of Italians or Spanish kids swarm up one side of the street, or occupy a coffee shop, and it feels like a benign invasion. But still, most of our local shops and businesses are managed by the same people who managed them seven or eight years ago, though now they commute in from the suburbs, since they can't afford to live here anymore. Meanwhile, the Brunswick Centre, a former council-estate, has been bought up and redecorated by top-drawer mega-merchants—Virgin, Waitrose and Yo Sushi! Oh no.

I've lived in many cities where it actually felt lonely to be alone, but this has never been true of London. It is a disorganized, uncoordinated, sloppy, disjointed, and counter-intuitive agglomeration of buildings where roads are always being torn up in every direction, and every pedestrian crossing feels like the most dangerous place on earth. Nobody seems to know where they are or where they are going, and every other person is feverishly consulting foldable plastic tourist maps or A to Zeds while looking more confused by the second. I can't blame them, either. After twenty-five years in London, I am constantly surprised by its depths, its diversions, and its interconnectivities. You turn a familiar corner and find yourself in a place you've never been before. Or abruptly realize that this bit is actually connected to that other bit you thought was miles away. London is like constantly being lost and found again. You walk into a strange conjunction of dilapidated buildings, turn a redbrick corner, and suddenly find yourself home.

So while I still feel California calling—the blue winter skies and wide-open spaces—I don't think I could leave London now if I tried. No matter how many flights I booked or trains I caught, I'm pretty sure I'd only be mysteriously tossed back again and again, like that guy in *The Truman Show*, eternally at home where I never belonged, waking up every morning to the same clocking clatter of trains underneath my bedroom, and the same outdoor smell of sausages.

Fanzine – 2007

Poetry? Funny? Hah!

[NOTE: This was originally commissioned by Chris Wiman at Poetry *for his first "humor" issue, which was scheduled for publication in the funniest month of the year–August. After sweating and stewing for several months on my deep inability to find anything funny about poetry, I eventually came up with this essay, happily sent it to Chris–and Chris just as happily rejected it. He did, however, pay me a two hundred and fifty dollar "kill fee," which only goes to prove that poetry may not be very funny, but that doesn't mean it doesn't* pay.]

LET'S FACE IT: poetry has never been very funny; and it doesn't look like it's going to get funny anytime soon. It's certainly established a pretty humorless tradition stretching back thousands of years.

Beowulf, for instance. I don't know if you've ever read it, but *Beowulf* wasn't funny at all. I realize the title *sounds* funny, but that's actually very misleading. Basically, *Beowulf* contains lots of glowering brows and dark forebodings and so forth, but hardly any jokes whatsoever. In fact, if you were to read this wholly miserable, so-called "epic" out loud (actually, I think I read the Cliff Notes version back as an undergraduate, or just enough of it to get by on the final) it's just really sonorous and apocalyptic, like being in church with your grandparents. And personally, I don't find apocalypse very funny. Or church. Or grandparents. But then maybe you do. Maybe you're even a poet–which, if we follow my thesis to its logical conclusion, means that you aren't very funny, either.

OVER THE CENTURIES, poetry didn't get any funnier. Like, say, "Dream of the Rood," which I think I also read back as an undergraduate, but then I drew a lot of absences that term, so maybe I just read the introduction. I definitely recall that it had to do with crucifixion, and personally, I don't find crucifixion very funny. Then, historically-speaking, there was this long lapse in poetry until we got to John Donne, and while I realize that some people actually consider John Donne quite funny (they may even have written their dissertations about him) personally, I'm still trying to figure out that whole two-legged compass deal. The only thing I did figure out about the two-legged compass deal is that it wasn't funny–not laugh-out-loud funny, anyway, which is the only kind of funny I rate. And while we're at it, people who write their dissertations about John Donne aren't very funny either. Not that I've actually met any of them; but then, I'm not looking to meet any of them. I've got better things to do.

Or take Emily Dickinson. What's so funny about Emily Dickinson? Buzzing flies and death stopping in a hansom cab or whatever, let's face it, the girl needed a man. I know that's not a very funny thing to say since, well, 1966 or something, but Emily Dickinson needed a man, and she definitely needed to get out of that house. Don't get me wrong, I'm not saying that getting out of the house (and possibly even laid) on a regular basis would have made Emily Dickinson any funnier, but could she have gotten any *less* funny? I think not. I think you see my point.

Things got continually less amusing up through the so-called modern age, so maybe we shouldn't dwell on it. Like Sylvia Plath and Hart Crane and John Berryman and those characters–how many laughs can you expect from a crowd like that? Sticking their heads in ovens and jumping off bridges and all that useless medication, I'm sorry, my sense of humor just doesn't get that dark. I like to laugh, but not at the expense of other people.

HERE'S SOMETHING ELSE that I don't find very funny about poetry, and that's poetry readings. How many times have you laughed out loud at a poetry reading–as in really busted a gut? It just doesn't happen. The best you can expect are these occasional moments when the poet makes a sort of joke–or what might be more accurately described as an "amusing observation"–that everybody classifies as "wry and clever," causing them to turn and smile and nod at one another in this very wry, clever, I-get-it sort of way, just so everybody else knows that they aren't stupid. But nobody actually gags on their pretzels or Teddy Grahams, or whatever cheap snacks are being served at this reading since (as we all know) poetry readings don't actually bring out the chow.

For example, when was the last time you laughed so hard at a poetry reading that you coughed punch through your nose? Never? But now think back to the first time you saw Jim Carrey speak through his bottom in *Ace Ventura: Pet Detective*. I'm pretty sure the first time I saw that immortally comic scene in a movie theater, I blew Sprite all over a group of kids in the front row. Now Jim Carrey speaking through his bottom–that's funny. Not that you'll ever see one of these holier-than-thou, egghead-types writing their dissertation on the subject. Oh no. It's all look-down-your-nose-time when it comes to Jim Carrey.

In fact, to be brutally honest (and as you can probably tell, I've been pulling my punches up to now), do you really believe that anybody with a decent sense of humor wants to spend sixty or seventy minutes in some tweedy little bookstore, numbing their butts on those uncomfortable aluminum folding-chairs, while pretending to titter at poems that aren't funny? Personally, I'd rather be a photographer for *Playboy*. I know that's kind of dated, and maybe even off subject, but wanting to be a photographer for *Playboy* has been on my mind a lot lately. Especially since I turned fifty.

Look, I like poets; I really do. I even like poetry, though I don't actually pick it off the shelf when I'm looking to bust a gut, or blow juice through my nose in an orgy of laughter, or anything like that. But let's face it, poets aren't a lot of laughs to begin with. For example, if I see a poet coming down my aisle of the local Stop and Shop? Well, I hate to admit this, but I turn my cart around and head straight for the parking lot, because the last thing I need is to hear yet another poet wittering on endlessly about how poorly their last book sold, or how they got screwed at their TPR hearing, or how that asshole at *Poetry Magazine* didn't have the brains to buy their latest (and, I might add, deeply unfunny) poem.

Poetry, I'm sorry to say, will continue being unfunny for an awfully long time to come—especially when you consider the current poetry crowd. I mean, have you ever brought up the subject of Jim Carrey to these people? They just don't get it. They look down their nose at you and get all "He's so crass and vulgar" and so forth. But no matter what they say, Jim Carrey talking through his bottom is still a hell of a lot funnier than, say, Robert Lowell's "For the Union Dead." Jim Carrey: funny. Robert Lowell's "For the Union Dead": not funny. It seems so obvious to anybody with half a brain.

Look, I'll tell you what's funny—any movie about forty-something guys who go back to college and live in a dorm—now *that's* what I call funny, especially if you had, say, Jim Carrey in it, or maybe that Elf guy, I never remember his name, that Will Somebody. For some reason—like they'll lose their inheritance if they don't or something—these guys have to sit in really boring classes about Beowulf and Emily Dickinson all over again, and go to dorm parties and frat parties, and watch beautiful young women climb out of swimming pools in soaking wet T-shirts and stuff like that, and maybe they start shotgunning beers and running around campus without any pants on and peeing in the Provost's pool, stuff like that, now that would be pretty funny.

Okay, maybe not funny to *you*–but we settled that already. You're probably a poet.

Previously unpublished

50+ (Not)

AT THE RISK of sounding ageist, genderist, and totally reductive, there's one demographic group I genuinely can't stand the thought of, and that's fifty-plus-year old heterosexual men who date. I know that's an unacceptably specific demographic to say bad things about, but I can't help myself. I'm a weak man who suffers from many irrational prejudices.

At the same time, I can't help feeling refreshed by this opportunity to openly bad-mouth anybody, mainly because I just don't get a chance to do it very often. For example, I couldn't get away with saying something similarly derisory about, say, female sportscasters, or Jewish lawyers, or Hispanic cops—or, for that matter, even fifty plus *homosexual* men who date. But when it comes to the unconscionable category of fifty-plus-year old heterosexual men who date, let's face it. Not many people are going to stand in my way.

Take me, for example. I'm a fifty-plus-year old heterosexual man who (with decreasing frequency) goes on the occasional date, and I have no problem with the idea that many people find me disgusting. *I* find me pretty disgusting. In fact, I'd just as soon not think about people like me.

It's a confusing demographic to get sucked into. And I certainly never got sucked into it by choice.

TRY TO IMAGINE this tawdry state of human affairs. Fifty-plus-year old heterosexual men attempting to pick up women in bars, or in coffee shops, or while surfing singles sites on the Internet. Or fifty-plus-year old heterosexual men going on Lonely Heart love cruises, or joining book clubs at the local Borders to discuss, I don't know. What sort of books would fifty-plus year old men discuss in order to get women to go out with them? Anne Tyler? Cormac McCarthy?

"Hey, I'm really intrigued by his stark realism in the face of existential dilemmas like love, suffering, horror and death."

"Really? How about a hot cocoa later at Starbucks?"

It's enough to put you off the idea of reading.

ARE YOU WITH me so far? Okay, then let's just say, for the sake of argument, that one of these fifty-plus-year old heterosexual men actually lucks out and wangles this proverbial date–what sort of horrorshow have we got happening *now*? He gets a haircut, shaves and puts on cologne. And if he thinks he might get lucky, he might actually buy bikini briefs or something ridiculous like that– because, let's face it, just about every conceivable thing a fifty-plus-year old heterosexual man could do to look sexy is going to end up seeming pretty ridiculous. Then he takes his "babe" to a restaurant or a movie. Can you even imagine a fifty-plus-year old heterosexual man taking his "date" to see, like, I don't know, *The Fantastic Four: the Rise of the Silver Surfer*, or *Shrek III* or something like that? I mean, they don't even make dating movies for old guys. Okay, maybe that new Michael Moore film about the health-care industry. But that's as good as it gets for a fifty plus year old guy and his honey.

I can feel you starting to get uncomfortable–as well you should do. But let's see this figurative misadventure through to the ultimate Ur-scene of our collective Freudian unconscious, and try to imagine, horror, horrors, that the date actually goes pretty well, and this fifty-plus-year old heterosexual guy actually gets his "babe" home and they start going at it. And, well, one thing leads to another.

Are you repressing yet? I know I am.

A fifty-plus-year old heterosexual guy trying to look sexy with his clothes off. Jesus.

I'm not getting that picture out of my head anytime soon.

ON THE POSITIVE side, it's not like many fifty-plus-year old men are either willing, or even eligible, to continue dating in the first place. Lots of them are already married, or remarried, or, even more categorically, divorced. (And let me tell you from personal experience–nothing takes the wind out of a guy's sails, romantically speaking, like a rough divorce.) Then you can figure there's at least a pretty decent share of guys who are mad, or religiously compromised, or have been castrated by industrial accidents and motorcycle-collisions, things like that. Or perhaps they've been shod with beeping ankle bracelets after a series of embarrassing court cases they'd rather not talk about–but whatever the reason, most of these old guys won't be bothering women with their unwelcome advances anytime soon. Also, let's not forget the rich and successful fiftyish guys (unlike myself), who don't need to go through the stress and trauma of dating, since they can hire high-class "escorts" from discrete procurers and so forth, or else screw their gold-digging secretaries in the conference room. Good for them.

So, as you can see, even a straw poll as sordid and halfhearted as this one would suggest that the world isn't about to suffer from a plague of fiftyish guys dating openly in the streets.

We, as a nation, still have a few things working in our favor.

I'M PROBABLY GETTING over-exercised about these issues since they've started hitting pretty close to home.

For example, I haven't been able to get my mind around the fact that I turned fifty a couple years ago, and ever since then, dating just hasn't felt right anymore. Every time I meet a woman I'd like to go out with, I feel completely embarrassed by any effort I might make to engage in conversation, or to smile flirtatiously, or to do all that pre-dating stuff I was never very good at even before I turned old. And even when I feel that little snap in the air indicating that I've met someone who seems even half as interested in meeting me as I am in meeting them, eventually I can't see anything but the same thought blinking steadily back at me from her (often beautiful) eyes, like a broken turn indicator at a roadside accident:

This guy's fifty-plus years old. This guy's fifty-plus years old.

And I can't blame her. Since that's exactly what I keep thinking, too.

NO MATTER HOW hard guys try (and from what I can tell, some guys try *really* hard), most of them just don't look good once they turn fifty. Believe me, I see them at the gym all the time, and even the ones who work out like mad just don't look very good. First of all, they're hairy in all the wrong places, like something petrified and forgotten you might find behind the oven. And for some reason I've never been able to fathom, they always seem to shave their heads like Bruce Willis, which is a fashion statement that has never made sense to me. But even when they're well-exercized, it all looks slightly wrong somehow, as if they've come unsprung in odd places, like those old family-room sofas people toss in the streets.

Basically, it's hard to act very sexy when you're fifty plus years old. In fact, you can probably only manage it with a fairly well developed sense of irony–and, as we all know, there is nothing less sexy than irony.

UP UNTIL NOW, I'm pretty sure we've all been in

general agreement: We just don't want fifty-plus year old heterosexual men acting foolish in discos, or carrying ribbony bouquets from the local florist, or waking up in strange bedrooms trying to find their way (with annoying frequency) to the toilet. (After all, why should fifty plus year old men be trying to achieve orgasms when most of them can't even pee straight?) We've all flinched inwardly at the unwelcome thought of fifty-plus year old men trying to sexily undress–unwrapping their raw crushed silk shirts and, excuse me, toreador pants or snug-fitting thongs to reveal pigeon chests, collapsing shoulders, and recent mammary developments–not to mention that peculiar dislocation that takes place between their thighs and buttocks when they walk. No, it goes without saying. We don't want to imagine that these people exist. Let alone see them parading their ridiculous new hairstyles and weirdly glinting jewelry openly in the street.

By this point, I have to admit that until now I haven't actually been dealing from the top of the deck; in fact, I've probably only enjoyed your unwavering (perhaps even enthusiastic) support by pretending to be gallant. But like the elephant in the room nobody wants to talk about, there's something just as disturbing as the thought of fifty-plus year old heterosexual men dating–and that's the equally unconscionable notion that many of these guys will end up dating fifty-plus year old heterosexual women.

I'm sorry. But it had to be said.

NOW, FOR SOME reason, a very nasty prejudice has settled into our nation, and that's that fifty-plus year-old men shouldn't "embarrass themselves" by dating attractive women much younger than themselves, and I can understand how this prejudice developed. If there's one thing worse than the idea of a fifty-plus year old man trying to act sexy, it's the idea that he might actually be doing it in the company of somebody who doesn't look half bad. But at the same time, this is not a workable prejudice. It doesn't even make sense.

For when you get right down to it, what would we, as a nation, rather see coming at us through the middle of a fragrant Manhattan summer evening–a disgusting old guy escorting an attractive, much younger woman who sort of lights up the neighborhood for a few seconds as she passes–or a couple of really old, dried-up, unsavory-looking characters, flirting and pawing each other shamelessly and so forth?

I think you see my point.

To sum up, it's unlikely that there's anything we can do–either through the courts, the ballot box, or some form of midnight-style vigilante-justice–to prevent fifty-plus year old men from dating. But if they're going to continue doing it, they should at least have the decency to do it in the company of much younger and more attractive women. Girls, a lot of this is up to you. You're going to have to abandon your prejudices against May-December romances, and understand that this isn't an issue of spending one or two evenings a week (however unpleasant) in the company of some much older, hairier, and smellier man.

It's an issue of public decency.

The New York Ghost – 2007

Orwell's Grave

IN MANY WAYS, Orwell's image has grown as eerily omnipresent as that of Big Brother. A tall, average-looking man with a two-day facial growth, loosely attired in dungarees and flannel work shirt, he either gazes frankly into the lens of his jacket photo, or averts his gaze just slightly, as if embarrassed by all the attention. His name, meanwhile, conjures up many abstract human qualities, especially to those who haven't read him. "Orwell," as in honest, brave, individualistic, and all that's good about the British people. "Orwellian," on the other hand, stands for everything Orwell spoke against. Totalitarianism, fascism, bad faith, and the dictatorship that would have resulted had either Stalin or Hitler won the war. By embodying his own contradictions, Orwell's presence on corporate-owned bookstore shelves assures everybody that the Good Guys triumphed. See, his books imply, freedom is the order of the day. Maybe nobody listened to him then, but everybody listens to him now.

Like Jack London, Orwell represents that moment in history when the airy abstraction of poetry came down to earth and walked like a man. It wore real trousers, drank real ale, performed real labor, and sensibly struggled in the wide, all-encompassing arena of *realpolitik*. And while Orwell's name may figure prominently on most A-level syllabi, students can usually get away with reciting a few fundamentals, such as that Orwell took "urban rides" into Paris slums, Yorkshire mining camps, and Spanish trenches, then went home and wrote memorable books about his experiences. In other words, he is more often remembered for being a great man than for writing great books. Orwell himself would not have welcomed this development.

The latest evidence that Orwell has become something of a monument to himself is the exhaustively researched, generally engrossing, and preposterously over-inclusive 20 volume *Complete Works of George Orwell*, edited by Peter Davison. The books are handsomely set and bound, cost a good arm and a leg, and are decorated with a foreboding, graffiti-like "O" on each darkly wrapped front cover. The cornerstone of this edition is an eleven-volume collection of Orwell's journalism and letters that, along with nine volumes of fiction, have been carefully edited to restore Orwell's "original intentions."

The first volume of Prose (Volume 10 of the overall edition), entitled *A Kind of Compulsion 1903-1935*, includes numerous childhood letters from the then Eric Blair to his Mum, schoolboy sketches, poems, playlets, and one particularly rousing tale of suspense entitled "The Vernon Murders," which was scrawled into a petty cash book while its author was still a teenage student at Eton. ("It was a stiflingly hot evening... The air was full of evil suggestions, of thoughts of murder.") These exuberant writings fill nearly a hundred pages of text, and require little more from the most devoted Orwellian than a fast skim. There follow a series of fragments that may or may not have been written during Blair's unhappy years in Burma's Imperial Police, and some sketchy early political journalism from his Paris apprenticeship of the late twenties.

By the end of Volume 10 (which contains more than three hundred letters, reviews, and even galley corrections), Blair has changed his name to provide a litigious-free byline for his first book, *Down and Out in Paris and London*, and returned to England where he earns his perilous living as a full-time writer. From this point on, he publishes eighty to a hundred thousand words of journalism each year, and reviews hundreds of books, films and plays over the course of a decade. The man we know of as George Orwell is born, and takes up his first residence in Grub Street.

These impressive volumes supersede the earlier *Collected Essays* edited by Ian Angus and Sheila Orwell. But where the '68 edition was designed to be read, the Davis edition is designed to be studied, and includes everything Orwell ever wrote, regardless of merit. Like many scholarly efforts in our Age of Information, the Davis edition never attempts to lend narrative coherence to its subject's life. Rather it simply files, lists, tabulates and indexes every available fact or document. It is not necessarily a "better" edition than the previous Collected Essays. It is just more comprehensive.

To give a general sense of how different the Davis edition is to its predecessor, it might help to compare some numbers. Where the Angus-Orwell edition contains 68 selected reviews, the Davis edition reprints all 379 that Orwell ever wrote, some of which only existed in typescript. The Angus-Orwell edition contains 169 articles and essays, some expurgated to provide clarity of subject; the Davis includes 263 articles without removing a single word or squiggle of punctuation. And where the Angus-Orwell edition contains 226 letters, the Davis stirs in hundreds more, many of which are as succinct and unilluminating as the following note to Cyril Connolly on 13 July 1942, when Orwell was Talks Producer for the BBC:

> Dear Cyril,
> Did Anand ask you about reading a poem in our forthcoming magazine program "Voice?" You might let me know as we want to get the program all sewn up as soon as possible.

> Yours,
> [Initialed] E.A.B.
> Eric Blair

Or this even briefer note to John Middleton Murray dated 12 April 1946:

> Dear Murray,
> Thanks very much. I'll be there on April 24th at 7.15.

All in all, the earlier edition contains more than four hundred numbered entries. The Davis edition, however, contains nearly four thousand, including lists of books Orwell owned, meticulous descriptions of his financial statements, fragments of uncompleted prose, and itemized notices of every time one of his essays or books was reprinted, translated, or condensed for *Reader's Digest*. In short, the four volume Angus-Orwell edition is solid enough to hold open that annoying door between the reception and den. But the Davis edition is capable of propping up the rear end of any mid-size economy car on the road today for a tire rotation and a lube.

AS THE FORMIDABLE data mounts, however, the question arises: Is all this additional material actually worth reading? And the answer is simple. Much of it isn't; much of it is.

If we stick to the year 1940, for example, the Davis edition provides many unexpected bonuses. For one thing, it transmits a genuine sense of Orwell's wide grasp and prodigious industry. For while most writers might publish occasional pieces on specific subjects that interest them, Orwell made his living as a journalist-for-hire, and freely reviewed anything that came his way. Detective novels, literary novels, thrillers, science fiction, biography, history, sociology, you name it. Books that were supposed to be good but weren't, and books that were supposed to be bad, but turned out to be a lot better than they looked. It was an excellent ongoing education for a man who loved books, and who possessed a healthy mistrust for the specious literary reputations assigned by what he called the "book racket." Orwell could not have found a better profession for allowing him to do what he loved: learn. He was not a man who liked to live with (or be ashamed of) his misconceptions.

It is also interesting to note Orwell's judgments on books by writers as diverse as Faulkner, Wodehouse, B. Traven, Nevil Shute, Upton Sinclair, and even Aldous Huxley, and to hear his thoughts about Chaplin's classic film, "The Great Dictator." The most impressive aspect of these volumes, however, is that, taken in their entirety, they suggest Orwell may never have written anything resembling a bad sentence. Though at times he can be rather summary in his judgments, he is almost never pretentious or vain. And even when he is dismissive, as in his evaluation of Denis Saurat's *Milton: Man and Thinker*, he rarely wastes words, and never neglects an opportunity to laugh: "This book with all its learning, does not remove the impression that Milton, considered as anything except a poet, was an uninteresting person." Orwell's opinions are often debatable, but unlike those of most reviewers, they usually seem genuine.

Some of the Davis volumes, however, prove pretty tough going, especially XIII through XV, documenting Orwell's years as News-Commentator for the BBC. In fact, after wading through all this administrative bamff, it is not surprising to learn that Orwell based his Ministry of Truth in 1984 on the years he spent trying to keep people informed on a government-sponsored radio station.

There are also times when Davis seems in too big a hurry to add a hitherto neglected item to the canon, such as his inclusion of an essay entitled, "Can Socialists Be Happy?" which was originally published under the name

John Freeman. "Freeman" is definitely the sort of nom de plume Orwell might have relished, and the essay does refer to many of Orwell's favorite subjects, such as Dickens, Wells, and Swift. But it is also just about the worst piece of writing in this entire edition, studded with the sort of wooden, thesis-driven paragraphs you might expect from a freshman comp class. Since Davis doesn't provide any compelling evidence that this essay must have been written by Orwell, the world could probably live without it.

But even when these volumes seem bloated and extraneous at times, they continually provide insight into Orwell's very sensible working life. He is meticulous in his record keeping, for example, and, unlike most novelists, competent with money. At all times his prose is rooted in the sensual particularity of daily life. And he seems as capable of running a review page as he is of changing a nappy, selling eggs at the market, or preparing his taxes. "I have a sort of belly to earth attitude and always feel uneasy when I get away from the ordinary world where grass is green, stones hard etc.," he wrote in 1936. For Orwell, even literary metaphors should have hard edges to them, and not drift far from the ground. The worst thing that can happen to anybody is to become, or believe in, an abstraction.

Like many critics, Orwell praised in other writers what he wished other critics might praise in him. Which probably why he developed an early appreciation for the banned books of Henry Miller. "The interest of *Tropic of Cancer*," Orwell writes in a 1936 review, "was that it cast a kind of bridge across the frightful gulf which exists, in fiction, between the intellectual and the man-in-the-street… Books about ordinary people behaving in an ordinary manner are extremely rare, because they can only be written by someone who is capable of standing both inside and outside the ordinary man, as Joyce for instance stands inside and outside Bloom; but this involves admitting that you yourself are an ordinary person for nine-tenths of the time, which is exactly what no intellectual ever wants to do" (CW, X, 499). To be "ordinary" was not contemptible to Orwell. It was something to which he aspired.

For the most part, Orwell's sense of fairness was his most rigorous attribute. He tried to respect the good work done by people he didn't like, and to like the sometimes-decent people whose work he didn't admire. (He even has a few kind words to say about Stalin and Hitler.) In contrast, it is hard to think of any contemporary left-wing scholar who would offer such spirited defenses of artists as ideologically diverse as Wodehouse, Dali, Kipling and Pound, simply because he enjoyed reading them.

The most controversial item in this edition is the list of "fellow travelers" Orwell provided the IRD in 1949, just before he died of tuberculosis. And it's possible he wasn't even moved by noble of motives–one of the people he named was an editorial consultant at Cape who rejected *Animal Farm*, and some of the others (Spender, Priestly, Steinbeck) sound like petty literary back-biting. But the last thing Orwell should be remembered for is perfection. There is certainly no writer who questioned his own motives more harshly than he did.

In the end, Orwell was not a statue in the park, but simply a man who had things to say and who said them as clearly as he could at every available opportunity. His novels were not always successful. His essays were not always persuasive. And his actions may not have always conformed to the highest ideals he set for himself. At his best, however, he never presumed to be better than he was. And at his worst, he wrote some of the best prose of his generation. This handsome new edition of his work provides an excellent opportunity for readers to go back and discover (or rediscover) his best work for themselves.

Times Higher Educational Supplement – 1998

Donald Westlake (aka Richard Stark): Quiet Man with a Fistful of Pseudonyms

AUTHORS AREN'T SUPPOSED to resemble the characters they invent, so it's no surprise to learn that the creator of one of modern fiction's most humorless, austerely professional criminals is himself amiable, funny, gentle and thoroughly unsevere. When we meet at his hotel, Westlake has just returned from doing post-production work on Stephen Frears's new film, *The Grifters*, based on a novel by Jim Thompson.

"On the way back to the hotel," Westlake tells his wife, "I wrote three sentences. Two descriptive, and one dialogue." Still in his fifties, Westlake has written more than 70 novels; it's very probable that he has written a fair number of sentences while finding his way back to hotels, or shopping for groceries, or strolling in parks.

Donald E. Westlake was born in 1933, and came to New York in the early 1950s, when original paperback fiction was a booming industry. Sold in bus stations and drug stores, the customarily garish covers of these books depicted rocketing spaceships, looming shadow-clad men with pistols, and seductive women wearing exceedingly obvious lingerie. It wasn't immediately apparent that these books were often both vigorously intelligent and entertaining.

Westlake published his first paperback novel, *The*

Mercenary, in his early twenties, and went on to write many more under both his own name and a variety of pseudonyms such as Tucker Coe, Timothy Culver and J. Morgan Cunningham. After nearly 30 years, however, the most enduring pseudonym has proven to be Richard Stark, the name under which Westlake published 16 certifiably "cult" novels between 1961 and 1974. *Aficionados* often refer to them simply as the "Parker" books.

"I never intended it to be a series," Westlake recalls. "In the first book, the police caught Parker at the end. But then my editor at Pocket Books, Bucklyn Moon, called and said, "Can you let him get away? Then you can write more books about him." So I changed the ending, and wrote more books." The first novel, *The Hunter*, was subsequently filmed by John Boorman as *Point Blank*, one of the most *noir* examples of contemporary crime-cinema.

Westlake wrote three Parker books each in 1961 and 1962, and then an average of two a year thereafter. "If I'd known he was going to be a series character, I would never have called him Parker," Westlake reflects, "because I could never get him out of a car. You can't say, 'Parker parked,' right? Sixteen books not being able to get him out of a car got to be pretty difficult. I had to start each chapter with him already out of the car, and ready to do business."

The Parker novels are notable for their hard, descriptive prose and impacted amoral glitter. Parker is the archetypal outsider, a freelance criminal roaming beyond the domains of organized crime–a mass of Waspish, faceless bureaucrats with names like Fairfax, Bronson, and Karns, quintessential organization-men who refer to themselves simply as The Outfit. Parker doesn't work for the Outfit, but only for himself; from crime to crime, he forges his own temporary alliances with other independent thieves, gun-runners and box-men, making his way in the world by playing his game according to his rules.

"I guess it all came out of growing up in the Fifties,"

Westlake explains, "when that whole monolithic America thought its society was now perfect, and therefore nobody should be different. Conformity and togetherness, and all that idealized stuff, and it seemed to me at the time like a society of ants. Everything was a given; there didn't seem anything to argue about. Being anti-social was a lonely business then. I just had this feeling, in my twenties, that if you had your own personality, you were like a cockroach living in a wall." And so he wrote a series of books in which even the most rebellious outlaw works and lives as methodically as any banker. Parker never feels anger or loneliness or doubt. He gets jobs done, hides his money like a squirrel, and moves on to the next caper.

Unlike the novels Westlake publishes under his own name–*The Hot Rock*, say, or his latest from Allison & Busby, *Sacred Monster*–the Parker books aren't intrinsically funny. Their humor is penumbral, rattling around just outside the frame of the action, as if the reader were eavesdropping on some vulgarly tasteful corporate boardroom; even when the characters are at their most earnest, the reader can't help but laugh.

Parker himself, who desires no friends, and who neither hates nor loves any of the women he sleeps with, functions not simply as the organizer of robberies, but as a sort of "people person," cold and calculating enough to imitate warmth and concern. As a colleague remarks, Parker knows to frighten his victims first, and then "talk to them, calm and gentle. Get their first names, and use the first names. When a man uses your first name, calmly and without sarcasm, he's accepting your individuality, your worthiness to live." It's not that Parker cares whether people live or die; it's just that killing is always messy, unprofessional, and of exceptional interest to federal authorities. It also interferes with his main objective: plundering armored cars, banks, sporting arenas, entire cities, and even island gambling resorts.

In *Deadly Edge* (Allison & Busby), the saga's

penultimate volume, Parker has even settled down; along with his mistress he has acquired a house, a mortgage, and some rather provincial money-laundering schemes. Like a remarkable number of American rebels and individualists in middle age, Parker is beginning to turn into his father. I asked Westlake if this didn't box him in, and he admits that since Parker's strange domestic turn, the authorial voice of Richard Stark has "gone away" from him. "I've tried a number of times to write another Parker book over the years, and one attempt I made was to open the book with the house burning down and Claire dying. But then of course I'm stuck with the problem that Parker's the last person in the world to go looking for Claire's killer."

This, of course, is because Parker's motives are never personal, but always purely business.

The Independent — 1990

Review of Comeback, *by Richard Stark*

SOME OF US have missed Parker, the quintessential anti-hero of contemporary crime fiction. A man of many names and few words, he possesses no family or friends, only business associates, and while he carries a gun, he doesn't like to use it unless he has to. This is because Parker is a true professional who goes about his work as efficiently as possible–which is, by the way, organizing heists. And the bigger the better.

Published under the name Richard Stark (pseudonym of novelist and screenwriter, Donald E. Westlake), the so-called "Parker books" first appeared as a series of Gold Medal paperback originals in the early sixties. The first of these, *The Hunter* (1962), was quickly adapted into the brilliant squeaky-*noir* Lee Marvin vehicle, *Point Blank*. And during subsequent outings (such as *The Man With the Getaway Face*, 1963, or *The Green Eagle Score*, 1967) the Stark byline developed a cult reputation for smart entertainment and straight-faced amoral irony. Like his contemporaries– Jim Thompson, John D. MacDonald and Peter Rabe– Richard Stark wrote quickly and for money, but the books he wrote have stood the weird test of time. In fact, if their influence on modern crime fiction and popular cinema is any indication, they have even taken on a life of their own.

The appropriately titled *Comeback* is the first Parker book in twenty years, but once you've read the first few pages or so, it feels like he's never been gone. Enlisted to help lift four hundred thousand dollars worth of "love offerings" from a Midwestern appearance of William Archibald and his Christian Crusade (like Parker, the Reverend only accepts cash and negotiable goods), Parker gets himself mixed up in a series of betrayals and turnarounds. His hired gun tries to pull a runner. The Christian Crusade's Chief of Security, a crewcut ex-marine named Dwayne Thorsen, starts operating a little cash-redemption scheme of his own. And one of Parker's confederates, a conscience-stricken member of the Angel Choir who sincerely wants to do God's work, accidentally sets in motion a trio of homicidal boobs named Zack, Woody and Ralph. In Stark's universe, it's important to remember that the second most dangerous person you meet is usually the good Samaritan. But the most dangerous person is always the amateur.

Parker is the archetypal American outsider, a straight-shooting, hyper-capable man who never takes anything personal, and who always keeps one eye on the bottom line. When he sleeps with a woman, he calculates how much she'll want for a payoff. When he steps into a building, he notes the ways in and out of each room. And when he wakes in the morning he checks the latest weather and traffic, stokes up on a high-carbohydrate breakfast, and sets off to steal all the money he can. "I'm not a specialist in people like you," explains a federal officer in an early Parker novel. "You're lucky," Parker replies.

A child of the Fifties, Parker doesn't like cellular phones, laptops, ATMs, or cyber-credit on the Internet. Instead, he prefers cold hard cash he can bury somewhere handy in a shoebox, and any gun so intimidating that he doesn't have to use it. This is because Parker isn't into abstract notions like winners and losers or profits and loss. Rather, Parker is into control. "What if I was the excitable type?" Dwayne Thorsen asks Parker at one point. And Parker replies, "I'd calm you down." Parker doesn't like to waste words for the same reason he doesn't like to waste people. You never know when you might need them later.

It's hard to imagine the contemporary thriller without Parker. A cat set loose among the corporate pigeons, he was one of the first fictional characters to extend crime fiction to big business (which is where, quite frankly, it belongs). And his influence on subsequent generations can't be underestimated, either. Elmore Leonard, for example, writes what he writes because Stark showed him how; and Tarrantino writes what he writes because of Leonard. This leaves an entire generation of writers and screenwriters prowling today's bookstores and movie theaters who are probably trying to write like Stark even though they don't know who he is.

It's nice, then, to find that despite his two-decade absence from publishing, Stark isn't content to rest on his considerable laurels, and as a result, in *Comeback* he is even brighter, faster and funnier than before. In other words, like his own most famous creation, Parker, Stark is the sort of consummate professional who's not afraid to learn from those who have already learned from him. He's prepared to do them one better.

The Los Angeles Times – 1998

73

Pulped: the Life and Times of Jim Thompson

JIM THOMPSON NEVER claimed to write capital-L Literature, but today, nearly twenty years after his death, many of his admirers are making the claim for him. Born in a sheriff's apartment over the Caddo County jail in Oklahoma in 1906, Thompson, like many good American boys, grew up to be a lot like his father. "Big Jim" Thompson Sr. was the popular multi-term sheriff of Caddo County until Oklahoma declared statehood at the turn of the century, and federal auditors began uncovering discrepancies in Big Jim's books. A warrant for the dishonored sheriff's arrest was issued and, after Big Jim took off, his devoted deputies refused to serve it.

In many ways, Jim Thompson grew up in his father's shadow, never managing to be quite so popular (or quite so loathed) as Big Jim himself–but this didn't mean Little Jim didn't give it the old college try. With his father absent for long periods (eluding arrest, making money to send home, or selling bogus oil rights to suckers), Jim dropped out of high school to support his family as a bellboy at the Hotel Texas, and quickly learned how to supply his guests with more than just the keys to their rooms. According to Thompson's latest biographer, Robert Polito, even as a teenager Thompson "moonlighted as a bootlegger, a drug peddler, a grifter, a pimp and a male escort." His extra-curricular activities often added as much as three hundred dollars to his weekly wage but, at the same time, demanded the sort of manic conviction and self-disavowal Thompson could only acquire through heavy boozing. As a result, he began suffering frequent collapses from alcohol poisoning and "nervous exhaustion." These breakdowns were to continue until the end of his frantically unhealthy life.

Like his father, Thompson began disappearing–from his wife and children, and from his jobs. He lived as a hobo, promoted get-rich-quick oil investments, read Karl Marx and dabbled in Wobblie politics. Then he buckled down for a while and worked part of his way through the University of Kansas, where he became the creative writing program's star pupil, publishing stories and poems in both the university literary magazines and higher-class publications such as *Prairie Schooner* and *Texas Monthly*. But after losing enough odd jobs to stuff the resume of any prospective novelist (stenographic temp, door-to-door salesman, bill-collector, oil-rig foreman) Thompson started making his living as a writer when he discovered the true-detective magazines in the mid-Thirties.

Thompson learned his craft as a thriller novelist by writing paid-per-word sensationalist exposes of supposedly "true-life" Middle-American atrocities, eventually mastering the sort of purple prose that kept housewives occupied underneath their hair-dryers, and commuters distracted enough to survive the daily grind of their trains and buses. ("The grisly crunching of an axe; the terrified pleading of a woman–choking, groaning. Then–silence!") The true-crime magazines paid him well for stories with titles like "The Illicit Lovers and the Walking Corpse," "The Ditch of Doom–the Crimson Horror of the Kechi Hills" and, my personal favorite, "Oklahoma's Conspiring Lovers and the Clue of the Kicking Horse." Like most schlock entertainment, true-crime magazines promised two things: cheap thrills and last-minute morality. The trick was to indulge readers with plenty of weird sex and violence, then lower justice triumphant into the concluding paragraphs on a rope. After the killers popped each other off in a rather bizarre double murder, or were properly zapped with enough state-funded electricity to illuminate Minneapolis, readers could feel that they hadn't simply read about terrible happenings–they had learned something about the inevitable connection between crime and punishment.

Eventually, true-crime magazines went the way of the pulps, and the ones that didn't go that way soon tired of Thompson. Moving his family to California, Thompson took a job cleaning plaster off the floors of an airplane manufacturer, obsessively reworked a few old manuscripts, and drank himself into several tizzies. The two constants of Thompson's life were drinking and excess; he did everything in bursts. He wrote in bursts; he drank in bursts; and when he made money in bursts, he spent it just as fast. After throwing his first unsalable novel out the window of a bus, Thompson made a couple of mad-dash trips to New York, hastily typed out some opening chapters and a plot summary, and with the help of Woody Guthrie, sold *Now and on Earth* in 1941. But despite a few good reviews–and two more novels published over the next decade–Thompson didn't hit his novelistic stride until the early Fifties. Again, in a burst of activity.

Between September 1952 and March 1954, Thompson published twelve crime novels, most of them with Lion Books, one of America's first distributors of original paperback fiction. Owned by the same company that produced Stan Lee's Marvel Comics and such slob-oriented monthly men's magazines as *Male* and *Stag*, Lion Books were, in their heyday, noted for their unapologetically tawdry cover-art and blurbs. Often retreating to his sister's bungalow at the Homestead Air Force Base in Dade County, Florida, Thompson didn't really write or compose novels so much as perform his narrative rage into the handiest typewriter. His first novel for Lion Books (and his best remembered) was *The Killer*

Inside Me, a tale told by a psychopath masquerading as a down-home sheriff in the Midwest. Thompson drew the plot for Killer out of a manila folder presented to him by his editor, Arnold Hano, but it was the last plot-summary Lion Books tried to hang on him. "You unleash a guy like that," Hano once said, "you don't try to direct him."

And unleashed Thompson definitely was; even the titles of his books testify to a terrible psychic venting: *Recoil, Savage Night, The Nothing Man, A Hell of a Woman*. In many ways, Thompson's books always carried his readers a little further into pulp-amorality-mayhem than they may have been prepared to go. Certainly his books never failed to deliver those goods touted on the garish tricolor covers—women trussed up on the floors after a beating, or buxomly offering bottled liquor to T-shirted men in dingy, claustrophobic bedrooms. On these covers, as in the novels, it was women who pursued men, while men shrugged anxiously with a sort of uneasy diffidence.

The women of Thompson's books don't mind a little rough stuff—not even when they're being beaten to death. After Deputy Sheriff Lou Ford finishes pasting Joyce Lakeland in *The Killer Inside Me* ("I backed her against the wall, slugging, and it was like pounding a pumpkin. Hard, then everything giving way at once,") Joyce doesn't try to run away or fight back, because no matter how bad he treats her she can't stop loving her man—especially when he gives her what she's looking for. What follows is a rather characteristic scene of Thompsonian sexual dynamics:

> She couldn't see; I don't know how she could. I don't know how she could stand or go on breathing. But she brought her head up, wobbling, and she raised her arms, raised them and spread them and held them out. And then she staggered toward me, just as a car pulled into the yard.
> "Guhguh-guhby... Kiss guhguh-guh—"

I brought an uppercut up from the floor. There was a sharp crack! And her whole body shot upward, and came down in a heap. And that time it stayed down.

IN *NOIR* FICTION, women operate as irresistible demonic forces. Once their passion is unleashed, men have got to either watch out, or take off the old boxing gloves and fight back with everything they have in them. This is because the human animal is, by its very nature, destructive; and since women are more "natural" than men (in the musky way they are described as smelling, or yearning, or purring, and so on) they are potentially that much more destructive. The men of Thompson's world (and this is true of most generically-bound male American thriller writers) prevail only so long as they can keep their lids screwed on tight, think straight, and not give in to any of those nasty old animal urges.

To survive in civilization, thriller writers like Thompson argue, men must disguise their basic animal identities. They must say, "Yes, Ma'am" and "No, Ma'am" at the appropriate intervals; they must treat their women like ladies even when they're really no better than, well, *women*; and they must go about their official "police" duties in such a cursory, affable manner that nobody notices they aren't getting anything done (unless, of course, it's some sort of secret mischief). Nick Corey, the high sheriff of Potts County in Pop. 1280, makes his career out of smiling at the right times, and talking like Gomer Pyle even when he's taking vengeful instructions from the Lord. And Carter "Doc" McCoy of *The Getaway* uses his face like currency, swapping smiles for confidences while plotting the murders of his business associates, or negotiating the sale of his girlfriend, Carol, to cannibals. Like the long- and short-con operators of *The Grifters*, "agreeability" is "a stock in trade." It's not who you are, but how you look. And you better look good, or else.

Thompson's male protagonists are evil, manipulative and utterly dishonest—and this is as good as people get in his world. Like Poe's Pym or William Wilson, Thompson's characters endure only so long as they dissemble; once they admit who they really are, they're reduced to their essential constituent parts—a spattering of raw flesh, an aimless cry in the dark. These are truly visceral novels. People carve each other with knives, collapse into bloody fragments, or, like the fleeing bankrobber-lovers of *The Getaway*, are "evacuated" from the anus of America into a Mexican crime-cesspool. The world is shit in Thompson's books; and the only way to prevail over life is by ending it.

The sudden demise of Lion Books left Thompson without a medium for his very peculiar message, since the only other prominent paperback publisher of the time, Fawcett Gold Medal, was looking for slicker, tighter stuff than Thompson could provide. (Gold Medal signature-writers of the time included John D. MacDonald, David Goodis and that thriller writer's thriller writer, Peter Rabe.) So during the late Fifties, when most of his proposed literary projects couldn't find a buyer, Thompson went on to do some of his best work for Stanley Kubrick's early films, *The Killing* and *Paths of Glory*. Thompson wrote a few more good novels—three of his best, in fact. But eventually, like one of his own characters, he descended into an alcoholic nonsense world. Even though he was regularly pursued by young male admirers who wanted to walk with him the mean streets of his books (without, of course, getting too involved) Thompson's writing grew more and more meaningless; and, as with Charlie Bigger in *Savage Night*, his body fell to pieces.

Thompson often derided Lion's "lurid titling and blurbing" of his books, but in many ways Lion provided the perfect package for his product. Like the so-called "gritty realism" of Lion's jacket art, Thompson's talent was for the shrill, excessive and vulgar—theatrical histrionics, *Grand Guignol* style melodrama, and enough bloody corpses to fill the stage of any revenge tragedy by Tourneur or Kyd. Like Tim Willocks, in a preface to a Picador reissue of Thompson's most famous (and often-filmed) novels, many of Thompson's readers were as impressed by the "way his name was printed on the covers–sleazy, dynamic and brash" as they were by his uncompromising genre-busting; and today the resurgent interest in Thompson's work has been sparked, at least in part, by a contemporary fascination with schlock as artifact.

Jim Thompson was a writer with real narrative energy. His best novels present a vision of America that is horrifically consistent; and he drove the assumptions of his preferred genre to their breaking point in a series of books that are truly *sui-generis*. But at the same time, he's a terrible narrative technician (unlike MacDonald or Rabe); the emotional hyperbole of his characters verges on the ridiculous; his misogynistic rage is continually embarrassing; and, with the possible exception of *The Grifters*, or even *The Nothing Man*, not one of his novels works as a sustained piece of fiction–which makes it difficult to accept much of the reverence lavished on him these days.

As an example of too much reverence and some devoted, energetic and intelligent biographical research, Robert Polito's new biography displays an admirable understanding of its subject, while assembling some exhaustively researched materials. At the same time, Polito seems to be arguing that Thompson wrote so bad it made him good. Or, in Polito's words: "Thompson detonates the clichés of the hard-boiled tradition he inherited–not by seeking to transcend them, as an important writer might be expected to do, but rather by sinking into the clichés so deeply that they are flipped on their heads." In other words, Thompson's often cliché-ridden prose is actually a "subversive" act–a peculiar argument when used to justify popular fiction. For while it is certainly true that Thompson triumphed in his particular genre–and took its often absurd basic propositions further than they made most people feel comfortable–it's just as hard to suggest he triumphed over his materials.

Polito's biography is a terrific piece of work–in everything but its critical justifications, which seem to be compensating for Thompson's stance as a literary "outsider" by trying to hard to drag him kicking and screaming into the established literary canon. And along the way, Polito makes a series of far-fetched comparisons between Thompson and Faulkner (both used multiple-viewpoints in their novels), Thompson and Beckett (both described "claustrophobic" landscapes), Thompson and Nabokov (both wrote about perverts), and even Thompson and Hemingway (both presented male protagonists who lost their penises in the war). It is impossible not to be intrigued by Polito's detailed attention to his subject; but it isn't long before you think that this attention may be a bit excessive. After all, it's not the literary qualities of writers like Thompson (and Philip K Dick and Goodis and Richard Stark, etc) that makes them so enjoyable to read. It's the alternative they offer to that which is supposed to be literary and serious, and that which is supposed to make us better than we are, which makes them so much fun to read.

London Review of Books – 1995

How Animals Saved the World: *Dr. Dolittle's Garden*

ANIMALS AREN'T SUPPOSED to talk; they're just supposed to listen. Sit, roll over, shake hands, play dead, get off the couch. They're supposed to do what we say, eat what we tell them, and unknowingly submit to whatever bizarre, outlandish tortures we devise–from slaughterhouses and dairy farms to petting zoos and high-class couturiers. So far as most human beings are concerned, animals possess value only to the extent that human beings can use them. Otherwise, they're just furballs waiting to happen.

Animals don't fare much better in the realm of fiction, either. Usually they're herded through simple-minded fables with tidy morals stamped on their flanks, or kitted up in top hats for cartoonish, minstrel-like musical numbers, or reduced to allegorical figures of nobly overworked proles and gluttonous, porcine bureaucrats. (Even a PC superstar like Orwell refused to let his animals stray too far from the farm.) In fiction as well as in fact, animals are expected to *mean*; they aren't allowed to just *be*.

The notable exceptions to such imaginative chauvinism are the books of Hugh Lofting. Published between the World Wars, Lofting's tales of Dr. Dolittle are among the most radically egalitarian in modern literature. They don't preach, allegorize or instruct; and the good Doctor himself coasts blithely through his numerous eponymous books without ever once telling anybody what to do.

The Dolittle novels are much like the good Doctor's garden–overgrown, unconstrained by human architecture, and filled with the generous noise and babble of various animals talking at once. For example, there's Dab-Dab the duck, who keeps a clean house when she's not waddling about it self-importantly. Or Cheapside, the wise-ass cockney sparrow; or Jip, the forever-loyal and hearth-bound dog (at least when he isn't off rounding up strays and introducing them to the communitarian ideals of Dr. Dolittle's Garden). And finally, of course, there is the perennially wise Polynesia, the ageless parrot who first taught the good doctor how to tell the difference between mimicry and speech: "You see, many parrots can talk like a person, but very few of them understand what they're saying. They just say it because–well, because they fancy it is smart, or because they know it will get crackers given them."

There is no sense of hierarchy in the good Doctor's back yard, where everybody comes and goes as they please, and where every animal, as Doctor Dolittle explains of his two-headed llama-like "pushmi-pullyu," is considered to be "its own property." The Home for Crossbred Dogs is located next door to the Rat and Mouse Club, and just down the road from the Badgers' Tavern and the Squirrels' Hotel. It's not a nasty, brutish, Hobbesian vision of Nature, but rather a Rousseauian, all-benevolent one. "The first and most important rule of the Dolittle Zoo," the Doctor's always-alert pre-teen amanuensis, Tommy Stubbins, records, is that "within the Zoo all hunting was forbidden."

The Dog Hotel features water bowls in all the rooms, sofas designed "so that the smallest dogs could jump up onto them with ease," and a bone-rack in place of the usual umbrella-stand. The Rat and Mouse Club publishes Cellar Life, a weekly periodical devoted to the best ways to identify good cheese and devious traps. And The Rabbits'

Apartment House consists of a large mound with numerous discrete burrows, not to mention the "community lettuce-garden attached."

Dolittle tends to animals, and does not master them; as such, he's probably one of the least obtrusive heroes in any continuing series. Throughout his many globe-trotting adventures, in fact, Dolittle doesn't really *do* anything. He doesn't train animals to perform tricks, but rather treats their wounds and restores them to the integrity of themselves. He doesn't yoke them to the braces of primitive farm equipment, but rather learns their languages and records their eccentric personal histories for cross-species posterity. Even when Dolittle invites his friends on voyages, he doesn't map routes or assign chores, but proceeds by means of something he calls "Blind Travel." This is an improvisatory parlor game involving an Atlas, a blindfold and a pencil.

Children may be the world's true anarchists, and in the Dolittle books (as in many books for children) authority-figures are usually represented as ogres, capitalists, and trolls. The only ideal life is a free one in which all animals are encouraged to speak openly about who they are and how they feel. (In many ways, Dr. John Dolittle sounds a lot like Dr. John Dewey, a popular philosopher of progressive American education at the turn of the century.)

At the time Lofting wrote these books, the world's languages seemed perpetually at war with one another. But in an ideal society, the Dolittle books argue, languages don't divide, they instruct. And if there's a parable at work in Lofting's unassuming and still-absorbing books, it's probably this: Don't heed parables; listen to voices. Then heed what those voices are trying to say.

(London) Times – 1996

Why the Beats Bite–Ginsberg and Kerouac

Review of Ginsberg: A Biography, *by Barry Miles*

THEY MAY NOT have been the best minds of their generation, but Allen Ginsberg certainly saw many of his friends destroyed by madness. David Kammerer, murdered in the park with a pocketknife by Ginsberg's roommate, Lucien Carr, then weighted down with rocks and dumped in the river. Jack Kerouac, who furiously drank himself to death at 47, living with his mother and ranting about communism. Joan Vollmar, shot in the head by her husband, William Burroughs, in the notorious, "William Tell" incident. Neal Cassady, who passed out after mixing booze with Seconal and died of exposure in the rainy mountains of Mexico. Suicides and Methedrine addicts, Buddhists and "criminal saints"–Ginsberg was more than a friend to the cranky, the hysterical and the odd. He was unabashedly and sincerely devoted to them.

Born in New York in 1926, Ginsberg's parents were refugees from pogrom-ravaged Europe, his father a respected minor poet, his mother a Communist Party member who suffered an escalating series of nervous breakdowns during Ginsberg's youth and adolescence. After his parents divorced, Ginsberg was empowered to sign the papers that authorized his mother's lobotomy; and it was probably this familiarity with the madness of someone he loved that drove Ginsberg to patronize the wild and frantic madness of poets, hustlers, junkies and thieves. Ginsberg did not simply love them; he kept them in his home, slept with them, found publishers for their often egregiously bad books, and declared them geniuses long after they were dead.

In many ways, Ginsberg was not simply a member of the Beats, but their chief begetter and champion publicist. "I'm with you in Rockland," Ginsberg wrote to his friend, Carl Solomon, in the haunting final stanzas of "Howl," "where you're madder than I am … where you imitate the shade of my mother." Solomon later denounced Ginsberg as a man who "enshrined falsehood as truth and raving as common sense for future generations to ponder over and be misled."

THE BEAT GENERATION (as in "I'm really beat, man") was never a specific literary movement so much as a supremely American democratic assumption–a dream of innate human reason, revolutionary truth, and the common man triumphant and revealed. "You don't have to be right," Ginsberg once said, "all you have to do is be candid." Reveal yourself in a shotgun splash of words and you were a poet, a novelist, a visionary, a saint. As James Dickey once complained, the "problem" with Ginsberg was that he made it seem as if just anybody could write poetry. Ginsberg and his Beats valued the raw stuff more than the formal clarity of art, as if the human spirit were a sort of vision-generator; their literary methods–the automatic writing they adopted from the Surrealists, or the more media-oriented "cut-ups" developed by Burroughs and Brion Gysin–were designed to encourage randomness and spontaneity. Anybody could be a poet; you didn't need to know form, metrics, fancy words; you just required enough potent humanity to spill onto a clean white page. "I have a new method of poetry," Ginsberg declared in 1952. "All you got to do is look over your notebook… or lay down on a couch, and think of anything that comes into your head, especially the miseries… Then arrange in lines of two, three, or four words each, don't bother about sentences, in sections of two, three or four lines each."

Oddly enough, for a generation that glorified freedom and license, the Beats took themselves awfully seriously. Ginsberg once claimed that while he was "absentmindedly masturbating" he enjoyed a visitation from William Blake, and subsequently ran around telling everybody else *they* were God. Neal Cassady, trying to break off his affair with Ginsberg, wrote him saying: "I'm not N C anymore. I more closely resemble Baudelaire." With just about every conceivable drug they could lay their hands on, Ginsberg and his friends set off to explore the deepest regions and contours of themselves—morphine, Benzedrine, laughing gas, mescaline, yage, methedrine, bhang, ayahuasca. As Ginsberg himself once wrote to Kerouac: "I've gotten so hung up on myself now it isn't funny anymore." He was right.

It's a hang-up Ginsberg never completely overcame; in a 1980 interview, he claimed that reading through his *Collected Poems* would be "like reading through Yeats. It will alter slightly perceptions of the world and open up space and tolerance and humor."

An early proponent of gay liberation, Ginsberg was disappointed by his first biographer, Jane Kramer, because he wished she had been "more realistic about homosexual situations," and Barry Miles has attempted to apply this "realism" to his kind, punctual and deeply respectful book. While Miles does not make much critical sense of Ginsberg's work, he does manage to amplify Ginsberg's formidable candor without ever lapsing (too obviously, at least) into hagiography. Relying on his long personal association with Ginsberg, as well as extensive access to the poet's private letters and journals, Miles has assembled a detailed, often florid account of Ginsberg's friendships, sexual relations, and political and religious adventures.

"Poetry is not an expression of the party line," Ginsberg once argued. "It's that time of night, lying in bed, thinking what you really think, making the private world public, that's what the poet does." In this case, the biographer does it too.

THOROUGHOUT FOUR DECADES of public life, Ginsberg's performative dance-card has always been full. Organizing political protests, dialogues with East European intellectuals, college lecture tours, and financial support for his friends and fellow poets; chanting Hare Krishna, performing rock music with Dylan or The Clash, activating his harmonium and finger cymbals at political and academic conferences, and trying to explain LSD to the Russians. At times, Ginsberg has resembled a poet of the world; at other times, he has more perilously resembled Shirley MacLaine.

Where Walt Whitman once catalogued landscapes of an expanding industrial society, Ginsberg assembled landscapes of America's just as rapidly expanding interior– the wide and immaculate world of the voracious self. It is probably no surprise, then, that Ginsberg remains America's most famous living poet. Americans respect candor, and Ginsberg, like America's other reputedly "major" post-media writers–Mailer, say, or Capote–has always proved himself an ardent self-publicist. Strangely enough, though, even as it gets increasingly difficult to enjoy Ginsberg's poems the further one gets outside adolescence, it is impossible to read this frank and unashamed biography without liking the very earnest poet who wrote them.

The (London) Independent, 1990

Review of Selected Letters: 1957-1969, *by Jack Kerouac, edited with an introduction and commentary by Ann Charters*

SMARTLY ASSEMBLED AND annotated by Ann Charters, this second volume of Kerouac's letters is filled with all the predictable excesses of spontaneous prose and dharmic bop: too much, too shaggy, too defensive, too sad. Beginning with the weeks leading up to the publication of Kerouac's second (and best-known) novel, On the Road, it carries on through his resulting incarnations as youth-spokesperson, celebrity, recluse, and drunk. "All I want," Kerouac once wrote, "is oldfashioned white bennies and a supply also of oldfashioned white phenobarbitol tablets to offset the benny depression 8 hours after ingestion (after 8 hours of writing)." It's no wonder that by the time Kerouac reached the end of his life he was so goddamn "beat."

Kerouac didn't sift and re-clarify his experiences so much as pour them raw into every available container. A man so obsessed with the past that from an early age his friends nicknamed him "Memory Babe", Kerouac produced some of his novels faster than most people could read, unreeling rolls of teletype-paper from his Smith-Corona in ten-day bursts of speed, booze, and self-congratulation. (He was especially fond of comparing himself with Dostoyevsky, Proust and Joyce.) The first thought is the best thought, he often claimed. And Kerouac certainly had more than his share of first thoughts.

"The act of composition," he once wrote his publisher

after discovering that copy-editors had allowed demon-punctuation to invade his jazz-novel, *The Subterraneans*, "is wiser by far than the act of after-arrangement, 'changes to help the reader' is a fallacious idea prejudging the lack of instinctual communication between avid scribbling narrator and avid reading reader, it is also a typically American business idea like removing the vitamins out of rice to make it white (popular)."

While Kerouac made his name writing happy novels about thumbing rides across America's vast highways, he didn't live a happy life in the confines of himself. And if *On the Road* neatly summarized his early wanderings with Ginsberg, Burroughs and Cassady, then perhaps his later years might have been just as aptly entitled *Sitting at Home Getting Drunk with My Mom*. It is certainly hard to think of a sadder late-career for any novelist: adding up daily word-counts of one's accumulating prose, waiting for checks and ticking them off in the accounts ledger, watching "The Beverly Hillbillies" on TV, and repeatedly dismissing former friends and lovers as Communists and Queers.

The greatness of Kerouac's best prose is all forward-yearning conquest of space and loving and time, but as these letters attest, he was a divided soul who often turned his brightest-burning fire against himself. "I'm on my own and always was on my own," he wrote a few weeks before his death by internal hemorrhaging at the age of 47.

It wasn't satori. But truer words he never spoke.

The (London) Times—2000

Going to Meet Richard Yates

RICHARD YATES WAS American's finest post-war novelist and short story writer, but he was a surprisingly difficult man to contact. He hadn't published a book in six years, and none of his books was in print in Britain. But in 1989 three were republished by Vintage's US division, so I rang them. I called four times without getting anywhere. Eventually, they gave me the number for a literary agent in New York, but it was long out of date. I called Vintage once more to ask if they were at all interested in helping me arrange an article about one of their authors. They weren't.

Eventually I tracked Richard Yates down in Tuscaloosa, home of the University of Alabama, where he taught briefly. I called him from my brother's apartment in Chicago.

"Oh, thank you for remembering," he said. His voice was gravelly, and he breathed with difficulty. "I've been ill, you see, and I may go into the VA hospital shortly, but I'd really like to do this, I really would."

The following day I called him again. He had just learned that his minor surgery was to be postponed for a few more weeks. This would permit a meeting.

I drove south, arriving in Tuscaloosa on Columbus's quincentennial, and Yates met me at the door of his bungalow apartment. He was tall, greying, slightly stooped and extremely cordial. For 10 years he had been suffering from emphysema, and recently the condition had grown critical. He was wearing a thin, semi-translucent green tube attached to his nostrils; the tube leashed him to a "Companion" brand oxygen condenser that he kept hidden away in the bedroom.

"It's not much of a place," Yates said. "But it's okay, I guess. Just for somewhere to hole up and finish my book."

It was a two-bedroom apartment with one bedroom converted into an office. Framed photos of Yates's three daughters were hanging on the main wall–Monica and Sharon, from Yates's first marriage, and Gina, from his second. (Both of these marriages, like the marriage of Yates's own parents when he was two years old, ended in divorce)

The only room with any real life in it was Yates's office, where a set of modular desk units were covered with scrawled, typewritten manuscripts. There was a large electric typewriter and a quotation from Adlai Stevenson taped to one wall. Yates was working on his eighth novel, which was going to be based on his experiences as Bobby Kennedy's speechwriter in 1962. It was long overdue.

"What I'm working on isn't really a very big book," he explained, almost with an air of apology, "but it's a very complicated one. I've been at work on it for six years, but of course this has slowed me down." He indicated the lengthy green tube that disappeared into the humming bedroom, but his loose, long-limbed gesture seemed to include a lot more–his life, his career, and this dull, leafy suburb of Tuscaloosa. "It's okay to hole up in to write, I guess," he said, "but I sure as hell don't want to die here. It's Dixie."

There's a lot out there, his gesture indicated, a lot that makes it hard to write these days. "I don't breathe too well," he said. "So all the oxygen doesn't get to my brain. I used to be able to write seven or eight hours a day. Now I can manage one or two, at best."

Yates's books are extremely emotional and not easily

summarized. Nor do they fit into any of the convenient critical categories: usually described as a "realist," Yates himself hates the term.

"All fiction is filled with technique," he complained. "It's ridiculous to suggest one technique is any more realistic than any other."

YATES'S FIRST NOVEL, *Revolutionary Road*, appeared in 1961 to generous reviews and disappointing sales. It's about the generation of Americans who, like Yates, emerged from the Second World War steeped in the illusions of Forties cinema and wartime propaganda about a glorious small-town America that never was: Mom and Dad and the kids, with an irascible grandparent or two thrown in around the fire. As in billboard advertising or television sitcoms during the Fifties, it's a family in which Mom solves all the problems with a faint, efficient smile of bemusement, and where Dad blunders ineffectively around the house and garden with his tools and gardening shears, never quite figuring out what those darn fool kids are on about. The kids, meanwhile, love Mom and Dad, sure, "but it's just like, jeez, Betty. They're so uncool."

Frank and April Wheeler, the protagonists of *Revolutionary Road*, are terrified they may actually belong in this place. They want to get out and journey to Europe to "find themselves"–if they don't leave right away, they might become just another part of what April calls "this enormous delusion–because that's what it is, an enormous obscene delusion–this idea that we have to resign from real life and 'settle down'. It's the great sentimental lie of the suburbs."

Like Frank and April, Yates abhorred sentimentality–in both his life and his fiction. He was also irritated by the convenient tags and labels that people were quick to attach to his own work. "It always struck me as a little too slick," he said. And for the next hour or two, whenever I asked him any "slick" questions, he shied away as if embarrassed.

"You're giving me too much at once," he said, with a shrug. Or: "I guess I'm just not smart enough to answer big questions about things like 'themes' or 'purposes' in my work."

The only aspect of his work Yates did seem inclined to discuss was his own disappointment with what he calls his "poor production." I asked him if he was happy about how his career had developed, and he replied, "Oh no, no, no. I should have written much more, about twice as many books as I have. But I had various problems over the years–periods of being blocked, having to do with so many other things to make a living and so on, teaching creative writing courses, or writing in Hollywood."

Despite the critical success of both *Revolutionary Road* and Yates's subsequent 1962 collection of stories, *Eleven Kinds of Loneliness*, he never made a living at his fiction until the mid-Seventies, when his long-time "roving editor," Seymour Lawrence, put him on a monthly salary. It enabled Yates to produce six excellent books over a period of about 11 years. But by the time of his energetic return to form in the mid-Seventies, Yates had already been dismissed by the critics as a "one-shot wonder." There was a long, painful lapse between *Revolutionary Road* and his second novel, *A Special Providence* in 1969. "I don't know what happened. It was the second novel thing, I guess. That book took seven years, and it had to be torn out of me." Yates's third novel, *Disturbing the Peace*, didn't appear until 1975.

YATES SEEMED MORE interested, sitting in his home that day, in asking questions than answering them. Where I had got my University of Chicago T-shirt, or what my brother did for a living, or where I was born, or where I was going next. Finally we broke for lunch, and there was something dimly Yatesian about how the rest of the afternoon developed–a constant slippage between intentions and effects.

At the door of his apartment Yates took a good deep breath and walked quickly to his car parked at the curb, where he hooked himself up to a large steel canister in the front seat. The car was littered with newspapers and food wrappers. I climbed in beside the canister. After adjusting his oxygen, Yates drove past the wide malls and shopping plazas of Tuscaloosa to a steak house, the sort of place his characters call a "nice" or a "decent place," which means moderately pleasant but affordable.

When we arrived, though, the restaurant was just closing, so we were forced to take second best–a large, vulgarly tasteful air-conditioned franchise restaurant called The Red Lobster. Yates attached his oxygen canister to a portable dolly and wheeled it with us into the restaurant. Over our beers we looked over the menus to see if they had steaks.

"Yeah, here they are," Yates said. "But they've only got the New York cut. That's way too big for me."

"So order it," I said. "This is on *The Independent*. Let's break the suckers."

"Oh no, it would be such a waste."

"You could take it home."

"You always say you'll take it home. But you always end up throwing it out."

We sank into the sort of transient, indefinite gloom that often infects Yates's characters.

"I'll tell you what," I said. "You order the steak, and then the part you don't eat, we'll throw it out on the freeway on our way home."

Yates ordered the chicken; I ordered a salad. We drank our beers and talked about the writers we both liked– Canada's Alice Munro, or Salinger and Fitzgerald ("If there wasn't a Fitzgerald," Yates said, "I don't think I would have become a writer.")

We were starting to relax and enjoy our "nice" meal. It was like the moments in Yates's stories when his characters stop fantasizing about romantic possibilities and start taking things as they are.

"You know," Yates said, halfway through our lunch, "This place isn't bad for a franchise restaurant."

When we drove back he was exhausted. I thanked him for his time. We had one more quick beer, then shook hands.

"It was very, well, enjoyable," he said, showing the sort of care with which he has selected virtually every single word of his published prose. Not a "great" afternoon. Not even "exciting" or "funny" or "wonderful." But "enjoyable," yes. It was very, well, enjoyable.

What Yates and many of his characters hate about the American "dream" of suburban fulfillment is its delusory, foamy blur. There's something about all the hum and buzz of advertising and movies, all those bright promises of the Best, the Greatest and Most Beautiful and the Love that Lasts Forever, which obscures and occludes the real and deeply-felt lives of our own hearts and muscles and lungs.

As Shep Campbell realizes at the end of *Revolutionary Road*, while contemplating his private grief over the death of April Wheeler: "The whole point of crying was to quit before you cornied it up. The whole point of grief itself was to cut it out while it was still honest, while it still meant something. Because the thing was so easily corrupted: Let yourself go and you started embellishing your own sobs, or you started telling about the Wheelers with a sad, sentimental smile and saying Frank Wheeler was courageous, and then what the hell did you have?"

After meeting a writer of Yates's talent and integrity, a man who never wrote a scene which didn't at least make a brave attempt at honesty, it was easy to think of him as "tragic," or "neglected," or as someone "who never lived up to his potential." But after all those "slick" observations are exhausted, the facts remain: he wrote some of the best fiction of his generation; and it continues to give pleasure to all those readers who are fortunate enough to discover it.

Three weeks after the interview, Richard Yates died in Birmingham's Veteran's Hospital, Tuscaloosa: emphysema, along with complications from the minor surgery that had been postponed. He was 66 years old. Remembering our afternoon in the light of that news, I do feel one slightly sentimental regret–even though I can hear Yates's voice in the back of my mind, warning me not to express it. ("Just tell what happened, and what you saw, and be done with it. And don't schmaltz it up with a lot of personal feeling, for God's sake.")   I can live with the uncomprehending publishers, the dumb reviews of his work, the dull place he ended up in, even the second-rate restaurant and the slow, awkward circuit around the driveway we made three or four times before Yates could find the exit on to the main road. I wouldn't want to change any of it because it was all enjoyable, really, a good day all in all, except for one little thing.

I wish he'd ordered the goddamn steak.

The (London) Independent, 1992

Obituary for Richard Yates

RICHARD YATES, ONE of America's finest post-war novelists and short story writers, has never been widely known in Britain, nor fully appreciated in his own country. Because his work customarily focuses more on people and emotions than on ideas and self-hype, he was the sort of writer critics rarely applaud but readers never forget.

Yates was born in New York in 1926, his parents divorcing when he was two. His mother, a sculptress, constantly moved him and his sister from one rented accommodation to another. Eventually, Yates left home to enter a rather shabby, financially questionable New England prep school, a period movingly recounted in one of his best novels, *A Good School* (1978). Afterwards, he joined the army and saw combat in the Second World War. When the war ended, he returned to New York, married Sheila Bryant in 1948, and began working half-heartedly at a series of routine desk jobs, earnestly teaching himself the craft of fiction in his spare time.

Yates lived a migrant life, and both his marriages ended in divorce. In the early Fifties he met his editor, Seymour Lawrence, who bought some of his stories for *The Atlantic Monthly*; Lawrence later gave Yates an advance that allowed him to spend nearly six years writing his first novel, *Revolutionary Road* (1961).

Revolutionary Road describes divorce and disillusion in the Connecticut suburbs. Tract homes, big green yards, children already, televisions glowing in the windows. Its protagonists, the Wheelers, dream of fleeing "the great sentimental lie of the suburbs" to go "find themselves" in Europe. Eventually, however, they begin to suspect they aren't real revolutionaries, after all; perhaps they really do belong in their unspectacularly pleasant tract house on *Revolutionary Road*. This novel was followed by a collection of stories, *Eleven Kinds of Loneliness*, in 1962.

In order to finance his next novel, Yates took a series of part-time teaching jobs in university writing programs, and went to Hollywood where he wrote an adaptation of William Styron's *Lie Down in Darkness*, which was never filmed. There followed a long, painful silence. Mired in bad jobs, writing blocks, and his own tendency to disillusionment, Yates did not complete his second novel, *A Special Providence*, until 1969–a novel which he later said "had to be torn out of me." It took six more years before his fiction got back on track with *Disturbing the Peace* (1975), a harrowing account of an advertising executive's descent into alcoholism and schizophrenia.

Despite poor sales and uncomprehending reviews, Yates's American publisher, Delacorte Press/Seymour Lawrence, provided him with a monthly income, and Yates settled down to his most productive period. *Disturbing the*

Peace was followed by *The Easter Parade* (1976), *A Good School* (1978), *Liars in Love* (1981, a collection of stories), *Young Hearts Crying*, (1984) and *Cold Spring Harbor* (1986).

Unfortunately, this arrangement ended when Yates's publisher went out of business in the late Eighties. Drifting again between temporary teaching positions and Hollywood, Yates spent the last years of his life working on a long novel about his experiences as Bobby Kennedy's speechwriter in 1962. Left unfinished at his death, it was entitled Uncertain Times, and while there is only a good chance it will still be published, there is an excellent chance that it is worth reading.

Even when his production was at its most infrequent, Richard Yates was never bad, and he was almost always great.

The (London) Independent, 1992

II.

Significant Others

i. Joseph Heller

Review of Closing Time

THE CATCH, OF course, is that there aren't many characters left standing to write a sequel about. By the end of *Catch-22* (1961) Kraft, Clavinger, McWatt and Nately have been snuffed out in various combat missions, Hungry Joe's been suffocated in the night by Huple's cat, Dunbar's been "disappeared" for threatening the lives of his commanding officers, and Kid Sampson has been crudely bisected on the beach by an Allied aircraft. According to Yossarian, who has pledged "to live forever or die in the attempt," anybody who wants you dead is the "enemy." And the enemy isn't just on their side anymore; the enemy is everywhere.

There are no fates worse than death in *Catch-22*, but there are a few that come close. For instance, there's Milo Minderbinder's rapacious M&M Enterprises, serving chocolate-covered cotton balls in the Mess or making profitable deals with the Germans to bomb Allied airfields. Or there's Major Major Major Major's officerial stage fright, or Doc Daneeka's lapse into bureaucratic zombie-ism, or even the harried Chaplain, placed under house arrest for stealing plum tomatoes and impersonating Washington Irving.

But probably the very worst way to go on living, Yossarian eventually learns, is to be accepted by the bastards who actually run things–the Colonel Karns and Cathcarts, the General Peckems and Dreedles. At the conclusion of *Catch-22*, Yossarian is offered a promotion and an honorable discharge, but only if he accepts this one little "catch." "Like us," Colonel Korn wheedles. "Join us. Be our pal. Say nice things about us."

Given this choice between dying or opting-in, Yossarian radically opts-out of the decision-making process altogether and sets off in the first available yellow raft for Sweden. Like most American fictional heroes, from Natty Bumppo and Huck Finn to Holden Caulfield and Randle Patrick McMurphy, Yossarian flees the world he's always known and sets out for places he's never been. It can only work out better that way.

It's something of a disappointment, then, to catch up with Yossarian nearly 50 years after the events related in *Catch-22* to learn that one of literature's premier escape artists has become the ultimate insider-trader.

Washed up on the shores not of Sweden, but of contemporary Manhattan, the greying Yossarian of *Closing Time* is working on his second divorce, attending Board of Directors meetings for the Metropolitan Museum of Art, and peddling influence for Milo Minderbinder's defense contracting firm, which is trying to sell the government more over-priced bombers it doesn't need.

Since the Second World War, Yossarian has been an arbitrageur, an investment banker, a public relations consultant, and a freelance writer (one of the running 'jokes' of this book is that Yossarian's always planning to submit another story to the *New Yorker*, even though they're always summarily rejecting him). He still runs after women, he confesses to his doctor, "but not too hard."

Now that Yossarian's on the inside, it's not so easy to laugh along with him at how crazy the world has got. The central "gag" of this novel, for example, is Yossarian's comic intention of staging an exorbitant wedding ceremony for New York's wealthiest elite at the Port

Authority Bus Terminal, which is infested with bag-people, women being raped in corridors, and people Yossarian refers to as "aspiring child prostitutes." When the wedding is held, in the novel's final pages, and after millions have been spent on oysters, haberdashery and sanitary engineers, one public-relations spokesperson exclaims: "This was the kind of event that makes one proud to be homeless in New York." He's not homeless, of course, and that's the joke. But it's hard to tell who will laugh at it, and whose side, exactly, they're on.

Closing Time stinks of a sentimental liberal piety masquerading as moral philosophy. Yossarian repeatedly bemoans the craziness and sadness of the world, and what a mess everything is, and how awful that we're all going to die etc, but underneath it all aren't we just glad to be alive? So let's dance, and drink, and make love, and blah blah blah, like Zorba the Greek dancing his heart out at Studio 54 and snorting designer cocaine.

Because *Closing Time* generates no comic momentum of its own, characters are always recollecting, in very stilted dialogue, major highlights from *Catch-22*. Consider the following exchange between Yossarian and Sam Singer:

> "You remember Snowden, then, Howard Snowden? On that mission to Avignon?"
>
> "Sam, could I ever forget? I would have used up all the morphine in the first-aid kit when I saw him in such pain. That fucking Milo. [Milo had replaced the morphine supplies with stock certificates for M&M Enterprises.] I cursed him a lot. Now I work with him."
>
> "Did I really black out that much?"
>
> "It looked that way to me."
>
> "That seems funny now. You were covered with so much blood. And then all that other stuff. He just kept moaning. He was cold, wasn't he?"
>
> "Yes, he said he was cold. And dying. I was

covered with everything, Sammy, and then with my own vomit too."

"And then you took off your clothes and wouldn't put them on again for a while."

"I was sick of uniforms."

"I saw you sitting in a tree at the funeral, naked… I saw Milo climb up to you too, with his chocolate-covered cotton…"

There is an awful lot of this sort of stuff. It goes on for hundreds of pages, like a Really Advanced Master Class in how not to write exposition.

Where Snowden's death in *Catch-22* recirculated hypnotically as a memory of the intimate blood everybody's afraid of losing, in *Closing Time* former events are ceaselessly recounted in order to remind people that a much better book was once written by the same author.

The (London) Independent – 1994

Review of Now and Then: From Coney Island to Here: A Memoir

JOSEPH HELLER'S MEMOIRS describe a vaguely nostalgic world already familiar to most readers. The streets are lined with low-cost tenement apartments. The multi-ethnic locals (who usually possess colorful "monikers" like Sammy the Pig and Mursh the Cripple) know the value of a hard-earned dollar. And non-franchise corner shops provide lots of modest pleasures, such as Golden Glow ice cream, or Mrs. Stahl's potato knishes. Eventually, however, mainland commerce arrives, bringing tourists, slummers, con men, and twenty-six flavors of Howard Johnson in its wake. The world doesn't feel authentic anymore. Suddenly it's filled with lots of crazy people only interested in making a buck.

Growing up on Coney Island taught Heller to suspect anything that glittered with false promise, such as the supposedly "gold" ring on the carousels that was really made of brass, or the beachfront arcades that continually offered flashy, unwinnable prizes. Such an abundance of "worldly knowledge," Heller writes,

> taught us always to look for fair value in money. We also learned at an early age a fact of capitalism that directed us toward the antithetical principle that it is usually impossible to obtain fair value. The difference, to Aristotle as well as Karl Marx, is known as profit. We learned first of all from the Coney Island barkers who offered to guess your weight, guess your age, guess your name or occupation, the country you came from or the date you were born, guess anything at all about you including the color of your underwear, for a dime, a quarter, a half dollar, or a dollar, the prize at stake improving with the increase in the amount bet. The fact was that the barker could never lose.

These early lessons are reflected most notably in Heller's first and best novel, *Catch-22*, where war is waged like a large-scale confidence game. Bureaucratically deployed violence reduces the meaning of human lives to aerial photos of tight "bombing patterns," while the captains of industry–in the guise of Milo Minderbinder's rapacious M&M Enterprises–reap huge profits for share-holders on both sides of the battlefield by serving chocolate-covered cotton balls in the Company Mess. As officers and enlisted personnel alike go mad, die, vanish out windows, or, like the harried Chaplain, find themselves placed under house-arrest for crimes as weirdly inspecific as stealing plum tomatoes or impersonating Washington Irving, only frantic Yossarian is crazy enough to see what's really going on. And that, of course, is blood. The blood of

Snowden, which Yossarian can't wash out of his skin or his uniform. Or the even more intimate blood that Yossarian himself is terrified of losing.

While reading *Now and Then*, it is hard not to be struck by the many ways Heller's early life influenced his work. What's infuriating, however, is how little Now and Then offers in the way of self-analysis. With the exception of a few brief descriptions of fellow Air Force personnel in Corsica who inspired some of *Catch-22*'s more memorable characters, Heller divulges almost nothing significant about his writerly life, such as how he wrote what he wrote, or why. And even when Heller does mention his writing, it is usually simply to point out how little he earned from his first published stories, or from *Catch-22*'s bestselling paperback edition. He certainly never offers a word of explanation why he wrote a sequel to *Catch-22*–*Closing Time*–that was so worthless.

This is one of the most reticent memoirs ever published by a significant novelist, on par with Paul Bowles's *Without Stopping* (which Bowles's friend and admirer, William Burroughs, once referred to as *Without Telling*). Heller certainly doesn't tell much–not about his thoughts, his feelings, his inner life, you name it. And whenever he does make reference to his family or friends, he usually sounds like he's brushing them off with half-finished clichés such as the following: "My mother, finding herself after six months of marriage a widow with three children, two of them not naturally her own, had brought us up as the mother of us all, and my brother and sister had related to her as such." When syntax gets this torturous, it seems designed to make things unclear. Never has bad prose looked more like bad faith.

TRIVIAL, EMOTIONLESS OBSERVATIONS mount up in this book to an oppressive degree, and at times it feels as if Heller has deleted anything interesting he has ever done or felt simply in order to maintain some false degree of composure. Usually, he describes places he has been, such as the endless train journey he took to his first factory job in Portsmouth Naval Yard, or the nondescript premises of every Manhattan-based Western Union Office where he worked during adolescence. His observations on life, meanwhile, insist on being incredibly routine. He "learns," for example, that "telegrams were delivered on foot" in the early 1940's, or that taxi license plates begin with an "O" and private cars with a "Z," or that it's impossible to just eat one pistachio nut–he has to eat the whole bowl. Eventually, even chapter titles belabor the fact that Heller is droning: "On and On," "And On and On," and finally even, "And On and On and On." As in Vonnegut's late novels and essays, the joke seems to be that Heller has nothing to say, and won't stop saying it. This joke doesn't remain funny for long.

Early on, Heller boasts that he has never shed a tear in his entire life. This will come as no surprise to any reader who has suffered the length and shallowness of these dull rememberings. If books were people, *Now and Then* would qualify as the sort of passive-aggressive personality that sits down in your house and dares you to like it. It refuses to be funny. It refuses to be interesting. It refuses to be tolerable. And it's so bland it doesn't even inspire the most short-tempered of readers to throw it out the window. In fact, the only response a book like this deserves is none at all. In other words–don't let it in the house. It will never make itself welcome. And it will never leave.

TLS – 1998

ii. Norman Mailer

Review of The Time of Our Time

IF ANYBODY DOUBTS the importance of Norman Mailer to the history of American literature, all they need to do is consult Norman Mailer. For example, in just the opening pages of this massive retrospective anthology of essays, interviews and fiction, Mailer doesn't waste any time setting the record straight. He dwells on his much-wished-for status as Hemingway's successor. ("I shared with Papa the notion . . . that even if one dulled one's talent in the punishment of becoming a man, it was more important to be a man than a very good writer…") He repeatedly characterizes himself as "a rebel against authority." And he provides lots of falsely modest self-re-assessments of his least-regarded books–such as his second novel, Barbary Shore, which he hopes someone will be reading "one hundred years from now." But *Barbary Shore* remains a dull, pedantic novel, even in such thinly sliced excerpts as Mailer provides here. And taken as a whole, this mega-volume simply doesn't digest.

Like most of Mailer's recent books (*Harlot's Ghost*, say, or even *Oswald: An American Mystery*) this book is too big and unfocused. This is because, as Mailer's introduction points out, it isn't limited to selections of Mailer's best work, but rather attempts to encompass the breadth and bulk of America. In other words, as per usual, Mailer's talent has gotten swallowed up by self-importance. Which, when you think about it, makes this book a fitting monument to Mailer's career.

At his best, Mailer is very good. At his worst, he is awful. What's most upsetting about Mailer, however, is that he has never learned to tell the difference. And whenever he faces the choice between saying what he wants to say, and trying to manufacture his own celebrity, he almost always decides to explore the least interesting character in all his books–himself. This is probably why Mailer has wasted so much of his career grappling with the likes of Monroe, Muhammad Ali, or even Madonna. He doesn't want to write about icons. He wants to be one.

As a result, Mailer was the perfect writer for our word-weary century. He appeared regularly on mainstream TV talk shows. He always told everybody what his books were about long before he wrote them. And he didn't invent stories or develop characters so much as embrace large (and, surprise, usually fairly commercial) subjects, such as sex, screen goddesses, and the Kennedy assassination. If you lived in America and watched television during the Fifties and Sixties, Mailer was the one writer you could enjoy without ever having to read him. You simply had to sit on the sofa with your evening cocktail and watch him emote.

Still, it is hard to regard Mailer's career as simply failed–it is a wasted one as well. And as this book shows, Mailer at his best is still worth reading, especially in his political non-fiction. Like many of the so-called New Journalists (Tom Wolfe or Hunter S. Thompson) Mailer transformed objective reporting into a sort of stream-of-consciousness journey into the true heart of American darkness–the utter mediocrity of politicians and their bushwah. A writer who continually strained against the superficial presentation of himself, Mailer was the perfect person to confront America's impacted amoral glitter, as in his coverage of the 1960 Democratic Presidential Convention in Los Angeles in which he describes the landscape thus:

> Not all the roots of American life are uprooted, but almost all, and the spirit of the supermarket, that homogeneous extension of stainless surfaces and psychoanalyzed people, packaged commodities, and ranch homes, interchangeable, geographically unrecognizable, that essence of the new postwar SuperAmerica is found nowhere so perfectly as in Los Angeles's ubiquitous acres.

Los Angeles, Mailer concludes, was "built by television sets giving orders to men." It is a perfect metaphor for the monster that America has made of itself.

Despite its bad faith, *The Time of Our Time* contains some very readable stuff, much of it previously uncollected, such as Mailer's thoughts on the Gulf War, or his unusually cool, unforgiving, and weirdly generous assessment of Brett Easton Ellis's *American Psycho*. And if nothing else, such a volume may at least refer readers to Mailer's best books of reportage, such as *Armies of the Night* and *Miami and the Siege of Chicago*. It's hard not to feel, however, that had Mailer used this occasion to assemble his best journalism from the past fifty years he might have finally produced the great novel people have been expecting from him—and that he has been expecting from himself.

(London) Times – 1998

Review of Oswald's Tale: An American Mystery

THROUGHOUT HIS SHORT life, Lee Harvey Oswald was a gun waiting to go off. His father, Robert E. Lee Oswald, died two months before Lee was born in 1939, leaving him and his brother under the dubious protection of his wife, Marguerite. Marguerite subsequently took up a number of awful jobs and even awfuller men, moved repeatedly from state to state and, when she couldn't afford to keep her sons with her, installed them for safekeeping in a series of orphanages, juvenile prisons and military schools. Lee slept with his mother until he was almost eleven; then spent the rest of his life trying to get as far away from her as possible.

It was Oswald's one prevailing passion to journey away from the country he knew. Growing up poor and poorly educated, he was cursed with enough intelligence to know he wanted more than he had, which meant that wherever he went became the next place he had to leave. Remembered by fellow classmates and social workers as a "non-participant," Oswald spent most of his young life alone in his room, rereading his brother's Marine Corps manual and dreaming about guns.

As soon as he turned seventeen he joined the Marines to put his dreaming to use; but the work was too hard and required too much discipline, so he spent most of his time shirking. He preferred to lecture fellow soldiers about the joys of communism, even though he'd never gotten around to actually reading either Marx or Lenin. Dishonorably discharged barely a year after enlistment, Oswald took his savings and fled to Moscow, where he turned in his passport at the American Embassy and applied for Soviet citizenship. When citizenship was denied, Oswald slit his wrists; when the government reconsidered and citizenship was approved, Oswald began planning his return to America.

"I am beginning a new life and I don't want any part of the old," Oswald wrote his family from Moscow, and it's a line that would make him a fitting epitaph. Leaving it all behind was the only progress Oswald knew how to accomplish, so he was forever saying goodbye for good. When he brought his Russian wife, Marina, back to New Orleans in 1962, he was already planning his next defection–to Cuba. And when he made his last, fatal departure from his home on 22 November 1963, he left $170 for his wife on the bureau, and his wedding ring in a cup. This time, Oswald left everything he had for the very last time.

Oswald never belonged, and by the end of his life he didn't want to. Like the copycat celebrities who came along since, from Mark David Chapman to John Hinckly, Jr., Oswald only believed in the existence of one person, and that was himself.

Norman Mailer makes many excuses for writing yet another book about Oswald (as he did about writing yet another book about Marilyn Monroe) but by the time you reach the end of this pointlessly long, egomaniacally lazy and poorly-written "mystery," it's hard to believe he was after anything but the bucks. "It is virtually not assimilable to our reason that a small lonely man felled a giant in the midst of his limousines, his legions, his throng, and his security," Mailer writes, in one of his few aimless stabs at a thesis. "If such a non-entity destroyed the leader of the most powerful nation on earth, then a world of disproportion engulfs us, and we live in a universe that is absurd." Mailer is arguing that by divulging the "real" Oswald, he analyzes the veracity of a nation. Like Oswald himself, though, Mailer likes tossing off big ideas, but he never likes to get down to the hard work of developing them.

The vast bulk of *Oswald's Tale* is nothing more than exposition lifted from other books–*The Warren Commission Report*, Edward Jay Epstein's *Legend*, Priscilla Johnson Macmillan's *Marina and Lee*, and so forth. And because Mailer can't be bothered to summarize important passages (it might mean reading them!) nothing is ever gleaned, or organized to enable readers to understand this complex story. In fact, the only original work lies in the book's first three hundred pages, which contain not only numerous personal accounts of Oswald and Marina's courtship in

Minsk, but KGB reports on Oswald's activities as an aspiring Communist and factory worker. (Again: like Mailer, Oswald liked the idea of work, but could live without the discipline of doing it well.) These opening pages offer some fascinating glimpses into Soviet life after the war, but rarely provide any insight into what Oswald was all about.

Mailer would rather copy out an entire page from a KGB report rather than simply state that Oswald walked around a lot in Minsk, visited many shops without buying anything, and often ate dinner alone. (Oswald was notoriously tight with a ruble.) Mailer will also present a two or three page transcript of a conversation between Oswald and Marina simply to prove that when they were alone they argued about dirty dishes and unwashed socks. Who knew? Who cared?

It's not the first time Mailer has preferred bulk to gravity. But it may be the first time he has produced a book as lazy and unproductive as this one.

Times Educational Supplement – 1995

Review of The Spooky Art: Some Thoughts on Writing

NORMAN MAILER'S CAREER has been largely retrospective. After his best-selling first book, *The Naked and the Dead* (1948), he went on to write two poorly received novels, and only achieved literary apotheosis with *Advertisements for Myself* (1959), what he calls "the first work I wrote with a style I could call my own." This featured a cocky publicity photo of Mailer in a yachting cap on the front cover, and was packed with Mailer's nose-thumbing reflections on fame, failure, and his fellow boxers in the literary arena. In other words, it was primarily about being Norman Mailer; and it began the longest serial melodrama in contemporary letters.

Since then, Mailer has published several retrospective looks at what he wrote, and what he never finished, and the latest has just been published in *The Spooky Art: Some Thoughts on Writing*. Mailer describes it as an "advanced" discussion on "the subtle perils and hazards of the writer's life." And many of its fragments, essays and interviews are pretty familiar by now: how Mailer fought his way through a combinatory haze of marijuana, Dexedrine and Seconal to make his "brave" final revisions on *The Deer Park* (a pretty bad book); how Mailer prevailed against the spiteful reviews of his Egypt-novel, *Ancient Evenings* (a really long, bad book); and how Mailer wrote a non-fiction-novel about murder, *The Executioner's Song* (a pretty good book) by taking a much different tack than that of Capote in *In Cold Blood* (a much better book). In addition, there are many lengthy and unsubstantive digressions on everything from "the real Brando cock" in "Last Tango in Paris" to the late-night despair of a TV addict (the book's best and funniest piece). All in all, it adds up to lots of good writing, lots of bad writing, and very little writing which has anything to do with the craft of writing itself.

The Spooky Art has been published to mark the occasion of Mailer's eightieth birthday, which makes this the time to say some nice things about its author. In the field of contemporary literature, where everybody shuffles about awkwardly as if they're loitering in church, Mailer has never been afraid to parade his bizarre, and often half-formed, opinions loudly in the parking lot outside. He has been both egomaniacal and self-effacing—often in the same sentence. And while his fiction never survived his youthful rejoicing in Dos Passos and James T Farrell, he has still managed to write some of the more perceptive and angry political journalism of his generation. Finally, Mailer often has interesting things to say about other writers, especially on those occasions when he bothers to read them.

For while Mailer likes to issue portentous statements

about the failures of American fiction since WWII, he doesn't seem to know what has been happening beyond the shores of his last Manhattan dinner party, or have anything to say about the many fine and lasting writers who were busily producing good fiction while he was lamenting its demise: Richard Yates, John Cheever, Flannery O'Connor, Alison Lurie, Charles Johnson, Tobias Wolff, J.G. Ballard, Diane Johnson, Brian Moore, or even– and this is the most peculiar omission of all–William Gaddis. A big ambitious book about America? Mailer doesn't seem to have heard a thing about *JR.*

And when Mailer does address the work of other writers, he can't seem to remember much about Toni Morrison except that he read either "one or two of her novels," or remember anything about the long productive career of Kurt Vonnegut, other than the fact that they often ate dinner together. He even addresses the issue of "style" in the work of Stephen King: according to Mailer, in one of this book's airiest summary judgments, King's style has "improved." When? In which books? How? Can you imagine Mailer being caught dead in an airport reading either *It* or *Gerald's Game*? Mailer can't quite elaborate on this remark, which is cited in the preface as a point of interest. He's too busy hurrying on to the next excerpt.

At his best, Mailer has flailed against the complacency of contemporary intellectuals; but at his worst, he has had a more lasting influence on bad writers than on good ones. In fact, his self-reflections often resemble a creative writing teacher's worst nightmare–that last dog-eared kid who comes slouching in late to class, buzzing with too much sugar or marijuana. He hasn't done the assignment, but he would like to share some urgent opinions about the merits of drug-use when jag-writing during an all-nighter. He insists that nobody can teach him anything, but he won't go away. And he doesn't read anything he doesn't have to–it might compromise his creativity.

Whenever I meet this guy (or girl), I always feel a bit

nonplused. He can't write; he won't read; and he just may be intelligent, ambitious and self-aggrandizing enough to win the Pulitzer. Or write a book someday about what he learned while writing.

(London) Times – 2003

iii. Steven Millhauser

Review of Martin Dressler: A Tale of an American Dreamer

IF WRITERS WERE judged by the integrity of their obsessions, Steven Millhauser would unarguably qualify as world-class. In his first two novels, *Edwin Mullhouse* and *Portrait of a Romantic*, he wrote about the compulsive desire of children to reread the same books, replay the same games, and revisit the same places over and over again. And in his subsequent collections, *In the Penny Arcade* and *The Barnum Museum*, his meticulously detailed stories described young men seeking every possible way out of the mundane world. In "August Eschenburg," for example, a nineteenth century designer of elaborate automatons eventually prefers his clockwork creations to life itself. In "Eisenheim the Illusionist," a Hapsburg-era magician vanishes into his own stage-managed illusion. And in "The Invention of Robert Herendeen," a lonely college graduate finds that the women he dates never quite measure up to his idealized conception of them (for one thing, they're much too bumpy). So after years of frustration he decides to imagine his own perfect woman into existence, and then a house to put her in.

Millhauser's characters would rather die than grow up–and many get their wish. Others live with their parents well into adulthood, or lose themselves in endless reveries, or disappear into the child-like stories other people tell about them. In some ways, Millhauser is a quintessentially Sixtiesish sort of writer, firmly placed among the likes of Barthelme, Barth, and Nabokov. In other ways, though, Millhauser's work is truly *sui generis*. For while his characters are obsessed with the magic of story making, they are never reduced to mere pawns in some elaborate metafictional game. In fact, Millhauser's fictions are very much about people, even though they may be the sort of people who spend too much time alone in their rooms.

Ultimately, though, Millhauser shares one powerful trait in common with the metafictionists: his books are purely literary. They take time to read; they belong on the page; and they don't easily adapt into major motion pictures starring Bruce Willis or Jessica Lange. As a result, Millhauser has received his fair share of good press over the years, but the best of his books have never been widely read, or even published much outside the US. His newest and best novel, *Martin Dressler*, however, has changed that. Along with the Pulitzer it won in 1997.

Martin Dressler concerns a young man who would rather reinvent the world than be in it. A tobacconist's son in late nineteenth-century Manhattan, Martin grows up surrounded by the seductive glare of commodity-packed department store windows, and dwarfed by the shadows of escalating high-rise apartment buildings. It's an age of limitless imagining, when financial empires are being built from inventions as innocuous as the bottle-cap, the tin can and the toaster, and the public is seeking a paradoxical combination of New World novelty and Old World comforts. For in an age of such impossible transformations, young Martin reflects, "People needed to be assured that they weren't missing the latest improvements, while at the same time they wanted to be told that nothing ever changed."

Martin, like all young men imbued with Horatio Alger-style determination, sets out to put his dreams to work. He invents a "cigar-tree" for his father's window display, acquires a job in a luxury hotel, and eventually wins his own tobacco concession in the lobby. He works his way up to bellboy, junior clerk, assistant manager, and with his secretly gathering bankroll, opens a series of franchise restaurants across the city–the first of which, quite appropriately, he installs in a bankrupt wax museum called the Paradise Musée. But as Martin's financial empire blossoms, he suffers increasingly edgy bouts of dissatisfaction and unease. The way things are is never quite good enough for Martin. He always desires more.

Martin takes nightly wanders into the expanding city, trying to imagine into existence something more profound and fulfilling than mere reality. He hires an Escher-like architect to design endless continuums of experience. And with the aid of an ageless young advertising genius, he communicates to the public his constant yearning for diversions. The purpose of window displays, Martin decides, is to lure people inside buildings. And the purpose of luxurious, theme-park-like hotels, is to make sure those people never leave:

> What seized his innermost attention, what held him there day after day in noon reverie, was the sense of a great, elaborate structure, a system of order, a well-planned machine that drew all these people to itself and carried them up and down in iron cages and arranged them in private rooms. He admired the hotel as an invention, an ingenious design, a kind of idea, like a steam boiler or a suspension bridge.

Martin doesn't just want to make a buck building homes for wealthy people. He wants to explore the infinite reflections of his own mind. Until, of course, he gets lost in them.

Like Beatty's *Bugsy*, or Welles's *Citizen Kane*, this is a book about the pathological American obsession with building things bigger and better than they already are. Fueled by Martin's infinite yearning, five-star luxury hotels expand into Gothically elaborate, Xanadu-like fortresses designed to keep people in, and reality out. And when Martin eventually conceives his magnum opus, the Grand Cosmo, it turns out to be an infinitely varied, constantly-shifting Borges Ian structure populated by seers, wild animals, secret Chinese masters, and bizarrely-equipped renegade metaphysicians. "There was thus a paradoxical sense," Millhauser writes, "in which the minutiae of the building were expressions of the architect's obsession with the gigantic, and a corresponding sense in which the sheer immensity of the structure was an expression of a miniaturist's tendency toward obsessive elaboration." In many ways, Millhauser isn't just talking here about the American desire to make new worlds of itself. He is writing about his own obsessive and richly detailed fictional creations.

Now that Millhauser's work has begun attracting the attention it deserves, it is possible to point out that his fiction, however absorbing, often feels static and confined. Because his characters continually desire some form of relapse (into childhood, imagination, dreams) they almost never develop compelling relationships with one another. In fact, nothing ever really develops in a Millhauser story; instead, images accumulate, mount up, multiply. As a result, Millhauser's narratives tend to lack any sense of forward momentum. At the same time, though, Millhauser has spent more than twenty-five years writing nothing but the sort of books he can't help but write. In an age when fiction is increasingly produced for the marketplace, there may be no higher praise for a novelist.

Times Literary Supplement – 1998

iv. Alison Lurie

Review of The Last Resort

IN ALISON LURIE'S world, nobody is ever quite as bad (or as good) as they first appear. Errant husbands turn out to be fleeing thoughtless wives. Plain, middle-aged women enjoy better sex-lives than their friends suppose (though their love-lives are a different story). And politically correct feminist icons eventually reveal themselves to be selfish, manipulative careerists who succeeded by sponging off men. Like Jane Austen, Lurie writes social comedies in which men and women circle one another in a bee-like search for honey. Sometimes they find the honey. Sometimes they don't.

Lurie's terrific ninth novel (or her "ninth terrific novel") is set in a Key West winter resort, where orchids blossom all year round, and countless short-lease accommodations are as transitory as relationships. Her protagonist, a "walking anachronism" named Jenny Walker, is one of the last surviving members of her species–the writer's wife. Married to the world-renowned naturalist, Wilkie Walker, a self-involved man nearly twice her age, Jenny performs his research, raises his children, entertains his guests, and schedules his engagements. She faxes, corresponds, edits, rewrites, bakes, and even keeps up with his e-mail on the Internet. Meanwhile, everybody she meets wants something from her husband, and talks to her as if she's a revolving door leading somewhere interesting. Still, Jenny is happy. She lives her life through her husband's work, and it's a life she enjoys.

Wilkie, on the other hand, has problems. Unable to get out of his own head for very long, he has attributed some recent rectal bleeding to not-yet-diagnosed bowel cancer. Not one to grow old disgracefully, he decides to take full advantage of this Key West holiday, by marching nobly into the sea to drown. First, though, he wants to complete his magnum opus, *The Copper Beech*, describing the sturdy, free-reaching life and eventual demise of a tree that bends and sways with the cruel seasons, blah blah. Wilkie has only one worry. How will poor Jenny cope with life when he's gone?

The Last Resort, like all of Lurie's novels, concerns men and women looking for some perfect partner, and then deciding they might be able to settle for a perfectly imperfect partner, after all. The title refers to the girls-only hotel run by an attractive, middle-aged lesbian named Lee, who sets out to seduce Jenny not simply because she's beautiful, but because she's read everything by Willa Cather. And in the space of a few short weeks, the displacement of one tenuous marriage sets off a series of chain reactions until just about everybody in town is looking for another partner. If there's one thing Lurie does brilliantly, it's describe the swift shifts that occur in emotional temperature whenever passion gets involved.

Lurie's characters is even more varied and engaging than usual. First there's the sixty-something, second-rate university poet, Gerald Grass, who's so tired of "cute" grad students that he's thinking about moving in on Wilkie's wonder-wife (after all, he could use a good copy-editor). Then there's the irrepressible Barbie Mumpson, who has flown south to reconsider her marriage to a sleazy political hopeful named Bob, who's been cheating on Barbie with a Las Vegas showgirl. Then there's Barbie's Mom, Mrs. Mumpson. She's loud. She's over-confident. And she demands that everybody in town should take her to lunch.

This is a book that continuously shifts its point-of-view. And as always in Lurie's fiction, point-of-view is little more than a style of misreading, as in the scene when Wilkie sees Barbie (who has just enlisted Wilkie's help in saving an ugly aquatic creature called the manatee) sunbathing by the pool:

> Wilkie had nothing against manatees per se, or even against Barbie–who, he thought now, somewhat resembled one. Like her the aquatic mammal was a little heavy, a little fleshy, a little slow; not too well adapted to the modern world. The manatee, however, caused no trouble to anyone: it rested in shallow warm waters eating water weeds. As he watched, Barbie's large-breasted, towel-wrapped (and thus apparently neckless and one-legged) form blurred in his nearsighted vision into that of a female manatee of the sort that sex-starved eighteenth-century sailors on voyages mistook for mermaids. And of course Barbie herself belonged to a declining species: the fans of Wilkie Walker.

For Lurie, point-of-view doesn't describe what a character sees. It describes who does the seeing.

The Last Resort is as good a place as any to start enjoying Lurie's remarkable fiction. And while it loses momentum in the last chapter or so (Lurie's not interested in the conclusions people reach in their romantic relationships–she's only interested in the dance) it is as funny, wicked, and smart as anything she has written. It also provides a sharp take on life in Key West, where love, sex and death are equally inevitable. Much like lunch with Mrs. Mumpson.

The Mail on Sunday – 1998

v. Steve Erickson

Review of Zeroville

STEVE ERICKSON IS that most unenviable of contemporary American writers–people either don't read him at all, or they read him too carefully for all the wrong reasons. More often than not, useless and misleading adjectives are applied to his work: "visionary," for example, or "mythmaking," or God help us all, even "Pynchonian." But Erickson isn't, to his credit, any of these things whatsoever. Rather he is, quite simply, a really absorbing and continuously inventive novelist. He creates unusual characters worth caring about–and he devises original ways of telling about them.

His latest book, *Zeroville*, is about as good as he gets. A sort of pop-culture-retelling of American history from 1969 through the early eighties, it follows the life and career of a renegade ex-Calvinist named Isaac Jerome (though he prefers to be called by the weirdly-appropriate name of Vikar). Raised without any of the usual cultural amenities--television, radio, magazines, and simple human affection–Vikar eventually defies his father by going to the movies. He has a disparate introduction to world cinema by viewing everything from *Blow Up* to *The Sound of Music*, and this turns out to be only the first step in an escalating series of transgressions.

When his father starts looking too intently at the kitchen knives and mumbling something about Abraham, Vikar splits for Hollywood. He shaves his head, imprints his skull with a tattoo of Mongtomery Clift and Elizabeth Taylor embracing in *A Place in the Sun*, and establishes a new home amidst the overheated landscape of palm trees, mansions, movie stars, and their directors. He hears rumors of strange families roaming the hills; he works as a gopher at the studios, and wanders with ghosts at the Roosevelt Hotel, Schwab's Drug Store, and the Houdini Mansion. Whenever he has a free moment, he scouts for meaning in the flickering frames of every film he can get his hands on–because, like Chauncey Gardiner, Vikar doesn't like to be. He only likes to watch. (So long as he doesn't feel like anybody else is watching back.)

Life is better lived at the movies, Vikar decides early on. For one thing, he doesn't have to worry about continuity so much, or one thing leading to something else he'd just as soon not think about, especially an ending–such as the one which haunts his dreams with the vision of a stone slab, ancient ritualistic writings, and a mysterious figure awaiting some terrible form of justice. In movies, Vikar likes to think, you can actually flee causality, the force that grinds Erickson's most memorable characters into the ground. "Each scene is in all times," Vikar often tells himself; "and all times are in each scene." For Vikar, film isn't aesthetics–it's ontology.

Nobody burns a metaphor into ash like Erickson, and the controlling image of *Zeroville* is the movie scene tattooed on Vikar's skull of "the two most beautiful people in the history of movies, she the female version of him, and he the male version of her." Vikar, labeled by one of his friends a "Cinéautistic," can only live and think through film; and sometimes, as a result, he can't tell the living from the thinking. Vikar's personal world is a giant movie theater without entrance or exit, much like the miniature church he designs in theology school and carries around in his pocket (or in his head). The prisons in this book are abounding.

In many ways, Vikar brings postmodern culture in his wake: the geeky slam-dancing kids at Madame Wong's follow him around like a pop messiah; DeNiro spots him at a party and bam, Travis Bickle is born; and eventually, Vikar burns his peculiar vision into the fabric of movies themselves. He becomes a film editor; he gets booed (and applauded) at Cannes; and he falls in love with the (purportedly) illegitimate daughter of Buñuel. He eventually starts stumbling across bits of his dream life in Godard, Hitchcock, Powell, Dreyer and yes, even Corman. It's not that Vikar wants to sacrifice himself for film; but he remains certain that somebody out there, maybe Dad, is still planning to sacrifice him.

Vikar's obsessions ultimately drive him–and his vision of the late twentieth century–towards a zero-point where they vanish into themselves; and, as in most Erickson novels, the narrative develops with so much persuasion and confidence that you don't notice when you've left the road altogether. In Erickson's first novel, *Days Between Stations*, the story journeys backwards in the life of an obsessive, Abel Gance-like director; and in *Tours of the Black Clock* and *The Sea Came in At Midnight*, his characters travel on a sort of möbius loop from history through self and back to history again. But in *Zeroville*, Vikar's story is not entirely regressive; he even triumphs, driving his obsessions to the point where he actually manifests them in the world of film he loves. He alters history. History doesn't just alter him.

Like the predictability-addicts and nullity-obsessed denizens of Godard's *Alphaville* (a film which haunts this book right down to the title), Vikar wants everything from life but love, and eventually he gets it. Shunning carnality, he fills his home with canisters of classic films; he moves freely through a world of film buffs and directors–Cassavettes, DePalma, Scorcese, and a John Milius-type who goes by the name of Viking Man. It's a life in which everything has been transformed into images—whether Vikar knows it or not.

In many ways, this all sounds more complicated than it really is—and that's the difficulty with discussing Erickson. His narratives are unusual, but not very interesting in themselves. Instead, they are always (and always only) a means of telling stories about the people Erickson imagines into existence—prematurely-aging children with a hard time understanding themselves, parents, history, and world. What makes Erickson most compelling is the confidence with which he wrestles these emotionally linear stories into existence; he doesn't compose new riffs on old stories, or bend different generic conventions into one another; and he is never merely quirky or surrealistic or gimmicky. Like most good writers, he genuinely believes in the narrative worlds he creates; he maintains them with consistency and conviction; and he drives them as far as they can go before falling apart.

And oddly enough, everything Erickson believes in as a writer seems to be what drives his characters mad: causality, obsession, vacuity, loss, aesthetics, movies, music and love. Erickson is always (despite his flaws, which can be considerable, especially in his longer books) genuine. He freshly examines the world each time he writes about it. And he reinvents his way of writing with each novel, testing his characters to the point where they can't be tested any more. He is the sort of novelist who keeps all the other novelists honest. And for these reasons, he remains much more interesting than the writers most people read.

Fanzine – 2007

vi. Cormac McCarthy

Review of All the Pretty Horses

CORMAC MCCARTHY'S FORMIDABLE prose is indebted to the Old Testament. His landscapes are wide, blazing and biblical with conflagrations. His characters are not thick, psychologically resonant creations, but always subordinate to the breadth and muscle of the world that surrounds them. In the Old Testament, of course, the surrounding world belongs to God. But in McCarthy's novels, it is nature—nasty, brutish and short. "I always figured they was a God," mutters one of *Suttree*'s Knoxville disreputables. "I just never did like him."

In McCarthy's existential landscape, men face two choices—to battle or die; the female characters, meanwhile, cook and sew or sell themselves on the street. There are times when McCarthy resembles a classic Thirties naturalist like Steinbeck or Lawrence, his characters commonly mired in the muck and muddle of their animal identities. But unlike the classic naturalists, McCarthy doesn't consider human beings to be corrupted by the civilization that contains them; instead they are the bearers of their own violent, irrepressible natures. McCarthy's characters tend to be murderers, indigents, liars and thieves; relentlessly brutalized by the world, they brutalize one another in turn. They lack the consolation of interior lives, suffering and surviving with a sort of indistinguishable vacuity.

The scope of McCarthy's first five novels is claustrophobic and messy. In his first two–*The Orchard Keeper* (1965) and *The Outer Dark* (1968)–men are casually murdered and a baby abandoned while a lot of whoring and drinking gets carried on in the white trash mountains of Tennessee; these first books read a little like Erskine Caldwell on crack. *Child of God*, published in 1973, proceeds into darker comic territory, telling the story of a serial killer and necrophiliac who is treated no less sympathetically than any other character in the McCarthy canon–which is to say, not very sympathetically at all. In *Suttree*, the eponymous protagonist abandons his wife, child and inheritance in order to live off his fishing, disdain regular employment, and associate with outcasts. He is Clint-Eastwood-laconic, which means he's a relatively dependable sort; in McCarthy's books, as in traditional American mythology, it's the educated, talkative types who are the most dangerous.

Despite their black comedy and often sordid melodrama, none of these books prepares the reader for McCarthy's fifth novel, *Blood Meridian*, a wide-screen, astonishing parable of the American West in which human beings chop, defile, massacre, maim and dismember one another in every conceivable fashion. It reads like all of Sam Peckinpah's late films edited together with the plots excised; the atrocities are rendered in such extraordinary prose that beauty is often indistinguishable from horror. This is, of course, McCarthy's point.

'A man's at odds to know his mind cause his mind is aught he has to know it with,' pronounces the judge in *Blood Meridian*, a satanic dispenser of wisdom and gunpowder. 'He can know his heart, but he don't want to. Rightly so. Best not to look in there.' For McCarthy, self-knowledge is a dangerous temptation; whenever his characters inquire into themselves, they discover nothing more lasting than the blood that spills from their veins, or the eyeless sockets that stare from their skulls. 'Your heart's desire is to be told some mystery,' the judge concludes late in the novel, before he has finished educating everybody straight into the ground. 'The mystery is that there is no mystery.'

In his sixth and best novel, *All the Pretty Horses* (the first in his projected 'Border Trilogy'), McCarthy attempts some things he hasn't attempted before, and mostly succeeds. The central protagonist is McCarthy's first certifiably 'good man', a 16-year-old boy named John Grady Cole. As the novel begins, Cole's history has just been yanked out from under him like a tatty carpet. His grandfather is dead and his parents have divorced; while Cole watches his father die slowly in a motel room, his mother sells off the family ranch. The solid world of work, family and history is being dissolved away by a world of supermarts and automobiles. Cole wants the old world back. The one he never really knew.

Cole runs away with a friend, Lacey Rawlins, searching for a land where he can ride his horse uninterrupted by fences, and where property is constantly improved through hard, honest labor rather than parceled off in lots. What Cole discovers, however, is the same muddy, awful horrors that destroy most of McCarthy's characters–bad love, dishonest cops, bloody conflicts, and people made dangerous by disillusionment. Unlike the characters in Faulkner (the writer to whom McCarthy is most often compared), McCarthy's people endure rather than prevail– if they're lucky; yet in *Horses* John Grady Cole approaches more heroic stature. Refusing to let the bloody world reduce him to meaninglessness, Cole seeks to attach some value to it, some formal signature. It is arguable that, by the end of this fine novel, he succeeds.

For the most part, *All the Pretty Horses* reads like the sort of classic western revisionism that can be found in films like Eastwood's *Unforgiven* or Peckinpah's *The Wild Bunch*.

McCarthy succeeds best as a writer about men and male friendships, and neither the love story at the centre of this book, nor the female character, Alejandra, ever really come off. But the prose, as always in McCarthy's work, is stunning, and the story far more absorbing than that in any of his previous books. As a result, *All the Pretty Horses* is the best place to start for anyone interested in exploring McCarthy's weird and violent fictional landscapes. It possesses both intelligence and integrity, and while the world it describes may not always seem real, it always feels realized.

(London) Independent – 1993

Review of Cities of the Plain

FOR THE FIRST three decades of his career, Cormac McCarthy labored solidly and obscurely in the field of American letters. He published well-written books that nobody read. He subsisted entirely by means of university sponsored grants and literary awards. And while residing in a succession of cheap Texas motels, dairy barns and minimally furnished cottages (one located next door to an El Paso shopping mall), he never showed much interest in either financial or critical success. His first two novels, *The Orchard Keeper* (1965) and *Outer Dark* (1968), featured backwoods coon-hunting hicks, incest, a rapidly decomposing father figure in the underbrush, and one very brutal campfire infanticide. Then, as if to prove himself more unpalatable to New York literary circles than canned chili, McCarthy published *Child of God* (1973), a short brilliant book about a serial necrophiliac in the white trash hills of Tennessee who kills people in order to love them, then drags them into his cavernous home to provide himself the perfect extended family—one that doesn't talk back. Obviously for McCarthy, being a shutdown

American male isn't a type of behavior. It's a metaphysical condition.

All the Pretty Horses tells the story of McCarthy's first certifiably good man, sixteen-year-old West Texan John Grady Cole. Set in the U.S.-Mexico borderlands just after WWII, Horses describes Coles's journey into a world more primitive and real to him than the dubious American prosperity he leaves behind, where ranches are being paved over by supermarkets, and sensible horses are giving way to insensible cars. In *The Crossing* (1994), an unrelated youth, Billy Parham, likewise goes to Mexico in search of things he can't bring back, and loses his devoted brother in the bargain. And now, with the just-published *Cities of the Plain*, Cole and Parham meet up while waiting for a new military base to close down their ranch and turn them into anachronisms.

Still relatively young, Billy and John have a lot in common. They like horses more than they do people. They've seen terrible things in Mexico. And during countless hours of roaming the wide landscape, they haven't exchanged any substantial information about themselves. In other words: now we have two good men. Which doesn't bode well for either of them.

Cities of the Plain is McCarthy's most laconic and understated book. While the trilogy's previous installments extended into the wide, still-bubbling spaces of post-revolutionary Mexico, this one sticks close to the border towns of El Paso and Ciudad Juarez, two grid-like cities laying snugly amidst a panorama of deserts, watched over by the brooding, stone-carved pictographs of prehistoric hunters. It's a wide, empty landscape where the primitive can still happen, and often does. Especially to those who think too hard about it.

Like most American stories about the friendship of men, things go desperately wrong the moment a woman gets involved. In this case, the femme fatale is a sixteen year old, epileptic Mexican whore, and from the moment he spots her across a crowded cantina, Cole decides to marry her. With the permission of his boss (another man wounded by love), Cole takes an old, roofless shack and turns it into a home. He arranges to purchase his woman from her pimp, borrows a suitable wedding ring, and even decides to sell his horse. Uh-oh.

In many ways, McCarthy is a classic thirties naturalist who doesn't believe in psychology. And when his characters have something to say it is usually about the nobility of animals, whom they admire for their abilities to perform physical functions without making too big a deal about it. As Cole argues to his friend, Oren, horses are basically moral creatures who know right from wrong:

> There's a way to train a horse where when you get done you've got the horse. On his own ground. A good horse will figure things out on his own. You can see what's in his heart. He won't do one thing while you're watchin him and another when you ain't. He's all of a piece. When you've got a horse to that place you can't hardly get him to do somethin he knows is wrong. He'll fight you over it. And if you mistreat him it just about kills him. A good horse has justice in his heart. I've seen it.

Which, of course, puts horses at least one up on human beings. Since human beings harbor plenty of injustice in their hearts. And can usually hide it from everybody, even themselves.

It is hard to think of a contemporary American writer more worth reading in his or her entirety than Cormac McCarthy. And while *Cities of the Plain* provides everything readers expect from him–it is funny, beautifully written, and *sui generis*–it falls flat in its concluding pages. As usual in McCarthy, the female protagonist isn't very convincing. And then, after a rather stagy knife fight, the trilogy trails off into the next millennium, during which a rambling epilogue belabors those themes that most readers have already gleaned. (Men are faced with choices between good and evil, truth and lies, north and south–which aren't genuine choices at all, but only vague suppositions.)

In other words, these books don't quite come off as a trilogy. (Though it's hard to think of an American trilogy since Dos Passos that does.)   But as three independent novels filled with considerable beauty and inspiring craftsmanship, they deserve to be read by just about anybody who loves words.

(London) Independent – 1998

vii. Irvine Welsh

Review of Filth

IN IRVINE WELSH'S Edinburgh, filth invests everything like a universal solvent. It percolates ominously in the bowels of corrupt policemen. It fills the streets with urine-splashed fast food containers and hastily discarded condoms. And it provides fast, convenient paths to every conceivable addiction, especially for drugs, prostitutes, pornography and beer. In a world of such constant visceral feeding, nobody has to think too hard about how they feel. All they really have to do is eat, drink, vomit and excrete. *Filth* traces the complete physical and moral collapse of Police Detective Bruce Robertson during a particularly miserable Christmas holiday. Assigned to the brutal murder of a Ghanian journalist and faced with either doing a good job or appearing to do one, he quickly opts for the latter course, and consumes his days cheating on overtime, extorting sexual favors from suspects, and routinely sleeping with every woman he meets. (In many ways, *Filth* reads like a Scottish version of *The Bad Lieutenant*.) Then, when time permits, he bolts down more sausage-rolls, masturbates to the latest Page 3 girl in the office loo, and returns home where it seems his entire family has mysteriously disappeared. Perhaps his wife finally got fed up with him, he decides, dosing himself with more cocaine and Glenmorangie. Too bad she couldn't arrange some sort of laundry service before she split.

Filth tries hard to be vulgar–if only to jolt its readers out of Robertson's terrible complacency. In just the opening chapter, for example, a half-conscious man is beaten over the head with a claw-hammer, the narrator releases a series of toxic farts (he refers to them as "Dame Judi Denches"), and, oh yes, there's the recurring problem of Detective Robertson's rash. Being an Irvine Welsh book, you can guess where that rash is located, and what happens every time it receives a good hard scratch.

In *Ecstasy* and *The Acid House*, Welsh chronicled rave culture's endless search for fulfillment, and in *Filth*, the same spiraling sense of addiction prevails. The more Robertson eats, the thinner he gets. The more women he sleeps with, the lonelier he feels. Until eventually the only company left to him is that of a blossoming tapeworm in his gut which, engorged by its endless diet of curries, Kit Kats and lager, possesses the one thing Robertson lacks– self-awareness. Before too long, this self-same parasite has even begun interrupting Robertson's story with its own peculiar brand of beat-poetry. Sure, tapeworms are awful creatures. But unlike human beings, they can at least be honest about their feelings.

In his first longish book since his brilliant and erratic debut novel, *Trainspotting*, Welsh continues to present a sort of "average guy" authorial persona, and nothing gets his dander up more than the liberal arts crowd. The most disgusting scene in *Trainspotting*, for example–in which the narrator staggers into an overflowing loo with a bad case of diarrhea and a much-yearned-for opium suppository–is entitled "The First Day of the Edinburgh Festival." And the closest thing to an artist to appear in Filth is the porn-merchant, Hector the Farmer, who videotapes bestiality while playing theme music from *The Archers* on his ghetto blaster. For Welsh, anybody who offers you a higher level of sensitivity than your own is a con man. Welsh prefers those who drag readers down into the roiling democratic gutter of themselves.

Like Henry Miller, Welsh explores the most extreme states of human behavior, but he often works so hard at shocking readers, that he puts himself in the unenviable position of having to beat himself at his own game. After a while, exaggerated comic scenes mount up meaninglessly, and even the funniest ones feel belabored. What's especially bothersome about *Filth*, though, is that while raging against everything artificial in contemporary life, it eventually purveys its own weird, half-felt sentimentality. Maybe the world isn't so bad as it look, Robertson begins to suspect; maybe he's just projecting a sort of deep-seated inner malaise. At one point, the tapeworm even argues that Robertson's sociopathic behavior may be the result of Thatcher's union busting in the Eighties. These oddly timed revelations and rationalizations feel terribly contrived.

Welsh is a sincerely fragmented writer who doesn't believe in either character development (his people never change) or plot (the meaningless universe he depicts never really leads anywhere). But when the picaresque comedy of this too-long book degenerates into a silly pastiche of Hitchcock's *Psycho*, it's hard not to feel cheated, especially since most of the "surprise" revelations were telegraphed in the first thirty pages. It's one thing to allow a writer as talented as Welsh to indulge himself in excessive bad-taste. But Welsh's avid, counter-cultural readers deserve more than a lot of phony, Agatha Christie-style plot-twists.

(London) Times – 1998

viii. Michel Foucault

Review of Foucault *by Didier Eribon, Tr. Betsy Wing*

THERE ARE PLENTY of good reasons to loathe contemporary French philosophy: Derrida's a prima donna, Baudrillard's putting us all on, Irigaray may actually be a little nuts, and both Althusser and Barthes have been run over by large motorized vehicles. The deconstructionists, meanwhile, continue to unwind recklessly tone-deaf sentences in order to refute their ability to communicate anything; the proto-Marxists deify the working class in a prose style that no upstanding member of the working class would be caught dead reading; and the feminists freely lift their terminology from practically everybody–Lacan, Marx, Freud–in order to glamorize their collective ability to speak the unspeakable. Confused? You should be. Too often, that's the point.

But while it's easy to get snow-blind reading most of this stuff, the work of Michel Foucault deserves special attention. That doesn't mean it's going to be easy: Foucault is a brilliant, convoluted literary stylist, but what he means is never readily apparent, perhaps because his philosophy challenges the very notion of "meaning" itself.

For Foucault, "discourse" is not a means of communicating information, but a strategy for deploying power. In his first major work, *Madness and Civilization*,

Foucault tries to comprehend how and why madness develops as a category of human knowledge in the 17th century. He doesn't analyze or define what madness is, but rather why madness is defined in the way that it is, and to what purposes. Foucault concludes that by identifying something called "madness," culture can describe the limits of sane behavior; these limits are then disseminated throughout society as scientific knowledge. By learning (and sometimes even contributing) to this knowledge of what is "normal," people establish the rules of who they are and how they should behave. Power is not simply force, repression, or imprisonment; it is a system of knowledge to which we all submit. This system is what Foucault often refers to as the "infrastructure of power."

In other words, knowledge is never factual or disinterested; it always enforces the prevailing systems of politics and commerce. To put this in a nutshell: Foucault sees all "human sciences" as an extraordinarily complex attempt to define the limits of the 'human' (in terms of sanity, health, knowledge, sexuality and so on). In more popular terms, this process might be called "normalization," and if you've ever seen photos of middle-America in the Fifties, you know what a frightening process "normalization" can be.

According to Foucault, we are all mired in the same oozy confluence of language, or what he refers to as "power-knowledge," a system of ideas, sciences, stories, theories and definitions which limit the possible horizons of human expression and endeavor. As far as Foucault is concerned, "individuality" is a term that prevents people from becoming, well, individual. He distrusts terms like "humanity" and "mankind," since they don't explain who people are but who they should be.

This goes some way towards explaining why Foucault's work is difficult, and why he avoids speaking in a "normal" human voice. But his writing is also brilliantly charged with complications, contrasts and endlessly unraveling subordinate clauses. Foucault was heavily influenced by Marx, Hegel, and the French *Annales* school of social historians, but he was never comfortable with any of them. Instead, he went back to Nietzsche and adopted his "genealogical" method, tracing the relationship between ideas and culture through the generations; he doesn't want to define what goodness is, for instance, but how it has been deployed. Truth is never permanent or ideal, Foucault argues: it is always determined by who uses it, and why. In order to learn, one should not construct edifices of knowledge, but take them apart. Sometimes, like Nietzsche, you use a hammer.

In his greatest work, *Discipline and Punish*, Foucault explores the ways in which modern systems of discipline do not simply surround people with walls, but invest them with knowledge. This knowledge instructs people how to dress, dance, eat, brush their teeth, hold their teacup and kiss their children; it prescribes normal ranges of fashion, architecture, sexual behavior and personal grooming. It can even be used to define acceptable ranges of the abnormal–avant-garde movements, say, in fashion, poetry or art. *Discipline and Punish* is one of the modern world's few essential books. It shows that if we want to understand how power operates, we must first question the deepest assumptions we have about ourselves. Like all great books, it confuses us about what we have always believed, and helps us understand what we've never known.

Because the individual is such a treacherous notion in Foucault's philosophy, any biographer faces some pretty severe theoretical problems. Didier Eribon has confronted most of these problems head-on, steering something of a middle course. He has chosen to write a concise, respectful, intelligent account of Foucault's intellectual life and development, while paying little attention to the human roar and muddle of how he lived when he wasn't busy thinking.

As a result, Eribon rarely dwells on the intimate, messy details–Foucault's hatred for his father, or the early years of frantic, near-suicidal despair about his homosexuality, or his personal relationships with lovers and colleagues. Instead Eribon focuses almost entirely on Foucault's intellectual life–his academic achievements, political activism, theoretical debts and allegiances.

You can't help but feel a little cheated whenever Eribon attributes a change in Foucault's personal life to philosophical differences–his sudden break with a long-time friend and colleague, Gilles Deleuze, in the mid-Seventies, or with his notorious friend and pupil Jacques Derrida a few years earlier. Eribon rarely considers human motives such as love, anger, pettiness, grief, dishonesty or sexual jealousy to have had profound effects on Foucault's life or philosophy.

Eribon's biography is good and useful work, especially in its depiction of France's fragmenting intellectual left during the late Sixties and early Seventies, but it seems a bit too supportive of Foucault's basic tenets to provide any critical muscle. It is also too respectful of his privacies to make any "human" sense of his life (which is obviously how Foucault himself would have wanted it).

Foucault resolved many of his personal contradictions by dismissing the importance of the personal in his work. He described systems of sexual and political conformity, but never spoke frankly about what he considered abnormal or embarrassing in himself. He had a great sense of humor, yet he wrote thousands of dense, utterly serious pages without a laugh. He complained about how institutions ruled contemporary culture, yet he was a devoted academician, and even involved himself in some of the reactionary educational reforms that led to the protests of May 1968. He called himself a structuralist until structuralism became the vogue, and then he said he wasn't one, really.

Eribon's biography of Foucault will be of interest to

Foucault's admirers, but it is not the place to start if you're interested in testing the frothy waters of Foucault's philosophy. If you want to learn how he thinks, you might try the essays and interviews collected in The Foucault Reader, which contains an excellent introductory essay by Paul Rabinow.

But if you want to understand how Foucault lived, and why he thought the way he did, you'll have to wait for a book that hasn't been written yet.

(London) Independent – 1992

ix. William Gaddis

Review of A Frolic of His Own

OVER THE PAST five decades William Gaddis has grown increasingly famous for writing big, impenetrable novels. His first, *The Recognitions* (all of 956 pages), met with hostile reviews in 1955, and nobody read it. His second, *JR* (726 pages), arrived 20 years later, received the National Book Award, and nobody read it.

Then, in 1985, Gaddis produced what some might consider his "breakthrough" work. Weighing in at well under 300 pages, *Carpenter's Gothic* marked a turning point in his career. For the first time in his life, Gaddis was unread for reasons that had nothing to do with length. From now on, he wasn't being read because he was Literature.

Like Henry James, Gaddis writes obsessively about the inauthenticity of American experience. There is no weight, texture or body to his America–only unraveling voices, buzzing radio-jingles, endless corporate hype and soulless legal blather. His people are always yearning for life's Deeper Meaning (art, truth, reality, self) but all they ever divulge is more money, commerce, lies, and junk. In Gaddis's best and funniest novel, *JR*, a 12-year-old boy masters the junk bond market by hiding behind a smoke screen of telephones, corporate logos and commercial hyperbole. In America, Gaddis complains, since the game is everything, it doesn't matter who plays it.

For William Gaddis, the American crisis is a crisis of representation, and it has produced a country in which prices don't represent value, language doesn't represent things, and politicians don't represent people. It's a place where money acts as a sort of universal solvent, reducing everything and everybody to the same smudged, greenish blur.

Gaddis's fourth novel, *A Frolic of His Own*, is about justice, and how impossible it is to achieve–especially when you're dealing with over-priced lawyers. "You get justice in the next world," one lawyer remarks in the novel's crisp opening sentence: "in this world you have the law." For Gaddis, the law is a system of language that doesn't refer to anything but itself. It never assigns guilt, innocence or value; it just keeps recirculating the same bad faith over and over again.

The central protagonist of Gaddis's new novel, Oscar Crease, looks to the law in order to regain the integrity of who he never was. Bereft of his father, his inheritance, and his art, Oscar decides to get even by demanding the only restitution available to him–money. Having managed to run himself over in his own car, he takes himself to court. Then he sues the makers of a Gettysburg-like movie for plagiarizing an old, unproduceable play he wrote, while moaning all the while that they didn't even bother to steal his best stuff (the film is directed by "Constantine Kiester" and stars "Robert Bredford"–in all his books, Gaddis's puns are intrusive and dumb). Suit leads to counter-suit until everybody's suing everybody else: artists and cities, husbands and wives, people and dogs. Meanwhile, Oscar hides away in his deteriorating family mansion waiting for what he's owed. It never arrives.

As Harry Lutz (Oscar's brother-in-law) explains at one point: "Every profession is a conspiracy against the public, every profession protects itself with a language of its own... till it all evaporates into language confronted by language

145

turning language itself into theory till it's not what it's about it's only about itself."

As in the work of Thomas Pynchon and Don DeLillo, the reigning narrative trope of Gaddis's fiction is entropy. Statements and actions are never completed; messages are lost and misdelivered; systems of information run down; discommunication reigns. People restlessly scout the wreckage of their lives for glimpses or "recognitions" of the original, the beautiful, and the true. But meanwhile forgeries multiply, and reflections usurp the place of what they are supposed to reflect.

By this time it's impossible to doubt either Gaddis's integrity or his conviction. His books are unclassifiable, unique, ruthlessly uncommercial, and demand to be read at their own speed–but at the same time, they usually go on far too long, and–with the blazingly original and nearly perfect exception of *JR*–don't entirely work. Like Hawthorne and Melville, Gaddis is fascinated by the allure of surfaces, and the inexpressibility of what may (or may not) lie behind them. But by writing about a world in which people take a long time saying nothing, the inconstant drone of Gaddis's characters often grows more monotonous than the world it's supposed to parody. Gaddis tends to repeat the same jokes, trope the same tropes, and obsess the same obsessions until most readers will eventually lose interest in the stunning architecture and simply walk away. About halfway through any Gaddis novel, even the most patient reader starts to feel like one of Gaddis's characters–bereft of everything but words.

Nevertheless, for a man who writes about a society washed over by cheap imitations, Gaddis remains one of contemporary fiction's true originals. He is funny, relentless and uncompromising. Not enough people read him–even if he is already Literature.

(London) Independent – 1994

Review of The Letters of William Gaddis

FOR AN AUTHOR who spent seven years writing *The Recognitions* (1955), a big, elbow-straining novel that most people didn't read, and the next twenty years writing *JR* (1975), an almost-as-big novel that most people also didn't read, it will come as no surprise that William Gaddis's selected letters are consumed with worries about how little money his books are making, how few people understand them, and how he plans to pay his bills until the next book comes along. As he writes his literary agent, Candida Donadio, in the mid seventies, just when *JR* was failing to secure a much-needed paperback rights advance:

> "America has odd ways of making one feel one's self a failure. And looking over the fragments of our correspondence assembled, I am just terribly struck at the consistency, from my end, of howls about money, and from yours of reassurances, hopes, encouragement: of course this isn't really news (and probably hardly unique in your file of writers), but seeing it so all at once did overwhelm me with a clearer sense of what I've put you through year after year, and I wish to Christ it had finally come up on the note of triumph you have hoped and worked so hard for."

Like most sensible serious writers, Gaddis never actually planned for his "triumph" to be posthumous; nor was he trying to write books that would be considered unreadable (usually by people who hadn't read them). "[W]hat pained me most about the reviewers," he writes in 1960, referring to *The Recognitions*' now notoriously-inadequate critical reception, "was their refusal–their fear–

to relax somewhat with the book and be entertained." To be fair, one can understand why your average reviewer might not have been able to "relax" when faced by a thousand page novel packed with theological allusions, inventive (but consistent) punctuation, dense, tiny typography and huge, tree-trunk-wide paragraphs. It's a daunting task just lifting one of Gaddis's best novels–let alone reading it.

As he writes Frederick Exley, a fellow writer almost as fascinated by failure as he was: "thanks ahead for your lectures on *The Recognitions*, that again is the God damndest thing: I've got about 1/2 dozen PhD theses on it also word latest royalty statement 5/5/81, $12.76, less 10% commission enclosed find our check for $11.48… that should inspire them!" For Gaddis, inspiration was something of a curse–it drove artists to do great things, and those great things often made them incomprehensible to normal people.

It's hard not to see the typical Gaddis hero in Gaddis himself–such as the young artist Wyatt Gwyon in *The Recognitions*, struggling to produce beautiful paintings in a world of forgeries, or the young composer, Bast, who bankrolls his artistic ambitions through shabby employment with a pre-teen junk-bond dealer named *JR*.

The weird part, though, is that Gaddis's books actually are entertaining, once they've taught you how they're supposed to be read. They are funny. They are moving. They are continuously inventive, and relentless in their obsessions–about forgery, and the meaninglessness of money, and the stupid convolutions of business-speak, and the frustrated aspirations of any artist who wants to create something genuine and original. The biggest problem for Gaddis was that his books required more time and attention than most people–and most critics–could afford to give them. You don't need a PhD to read *JR*, or a critical concordance; you just need a secluded island somewhere, without Cable or Satellite TV. You need time.

(Oh yeah, and a sense of humor. It's hilarious.)

"[A] sense of humor is simply a sense of proportion," he writes his daughter, the soon-to-be-novelist, Sarah Gaddis, shortly after his first divorce, "of the real worth of things in relation to each other, which lets you see how totally ridiculous some of the most intensely fought out selfish battles can often be, and Sarah if you can keep your sense of humor you are a step ahead almost everywhere you go."

As a young man freshly ejected from Harvard for drunken behavior, Gaddis took a series of road trips, during which he reported back in great detail to his mother; these long freewheeling beat-like narrative riffs across American space were the testing grounds for both Gaddis's style, and his ontology. "While the world of fact drowns us," he writes on approaching Laredo, Texas, "that of probability supplies an occasional bubble of life, and we plan…" For Gaddis, America is an inundation of extraneous facts and information: money, pop culture, business jargon, hack politicians, stupid celebrities, and always-hustling con men and con women. The great risk of America is that there is just too damned much of it, and most of it is ugly and meretricious.

It's not surprising that Gaddis bristled whenever he was labeled "experimental," a term which, Gaddis wrote late in his life, he found "specifically unsuited, due to my sense of the decline in the use and meaning of 'experimental' and 'experiment' from the blunt dictionary definition as 'A test made to demonstrate a known truth' to which I should happily subscribe, to the rather loose embrace of writing pursued willy-nilly in some fond hope of stumbling on those strokes of brilliance which that perfect poet Keats mistrusted even in himself…" Like Faulkner, Gaddis only "experimented" in order to confirm those very conventional pleasures inherent in any good novel: that narrative webwork of human life and human language and the always noisily beautiful discord of people.

As Gaddis's friend, Stanley Elkin, remarked: *JR* is the sort of book that you "hear with your eyes." Four words. That was all it took. One of the best reviews Gaddis ever received from someone who had actually read him.

But despite the absence of anything that might resemble a critical "triumph" in Gaddis's life, he did seem to enjoy his slow steady ascent into the light before he passed away from prostate cancer in 1998. Eventually, he wrote a book that was short enough to be read by more than just a few highly attentive and patient people (*Carpenter's Gothic*); he won awards–the National Book Award, the MacArthur "genius grant", and the Lannan Literary Award for Lifetime Achievement. And he even lived long enough to see *The Recognitions* brought back into print in a relatively error-free edition. He even seemed to enjoy his career for a while, received a couple decent advances, and grew slightly less concerned with money. He watched his two children, whom he clearly loved, grow up. ("You each give me more to be proud of than *JR*. (Throw in *The Recognitions* too.)" He even may have eventually convinced some people that he never actually read the book that was most often cited as his major influence. ("I recall a most ingenious piece in a Wisconsin quarterly some years ago," he writes an enquiring student, "in which *The Recognitions'* debt to *Ulysses* was established in such minute detail I was doubtful of my own firm recollection of never having read *Ulysses*…") He never loses his sense of humor, or his sense of proportion. And he keeps working, and creating beautiful sentences, until the end.

New York Times Book Review – 2013

x. Colson Whitehead

Review of Apex Hides the Hurt

LIKE RALPH ELLISON and Richard Wright, Colson Whitehead doesn't see "blackness" as the existential crisis to be overcome by many Americans–it is simply one in a series of related crises: those that are acted out each day in the arena of a vast, articulate culture that wants to define people, regardless of race, gender, or ability, before they have a chance to define themselves. In other words, identity isn't a matter of pigmentation, but of perception– as in how keenly you read (or misread) others. And in how keenly they read (or misread) you.

Whitehead's characters suffer from a sort of social dyslexia. Unable to make sense of the world around them, they often stop trying. They work at dead-end jobs for large, faceless corporations, establish few (if any) lasting relationships, and waste their days haunting anonymous urban landscapes and franchise-hotel restaurants, pondering the essential meaninglessness of elevators, postage stamps, and brand names. Even their professional skills don't make them happy, but only increase their feelings of isolation, alienation, and regret.

In *The Intuitionist*, for example, Lila Mae Watson can "sense," like some Industrial Age machine whisperer, when an elevator may not actually go up and down as scheduled. And in *John Henry Days*, freelance hack J. Sutter

SCOTT BRADFIELD

makes a precarious living going on press junkets, collecting other people's reimbursable expense receipts, and producing decent ad copy that looks like bad journalism (or bad journalism that looks like decent ad copy–he's not entirely sure).

The protagonist of Whitehead's third novel, *Apex Hides the Hurt*, is a hot young "nomenclature consultant" (purposely left unnamed) who possesses a knack for signification. When clients need to launch (or relaunch) a commercial product, they hire him to slap on the only thing that matters–a shiny new brand name. Sometimes, the stuff they're touting is medicinal: Drowsatin, say, for sleeping your cares away, or StaySlim for those who, well, you know, can't. Other times, it's recreational, such as Brio, the energy drink for people who stay up late staring at computers, or Outfit Outlet and Admiral Java, two of those omnipresent mall stops where lonely consumers go to share in the communal experience of buying.

But whether they come in the form of an ointment, a gel, or a latte, it's not the products themselves but only their brightly labeled packages that seem to relieve people of their pain. Which is probably why the man with the naming touch doesn't think of himself as a salesman; he considers himself more an oracle or a prophet:

> It was the kind of business where there were a lot of Eureka stories. Much of the work went on in the subconscious level. He was making connections between things without thinking and then, bam on the subway scratching a nose, or bam bam while stubbing a toe on the curb. Floating in neon before him was the name. When the products flopped, he told himself it was because of the marketing people. It was the stupid public. The crap-ass thing itself. Never the name because what he did was perfect.

152

For the protagonist, names are a primordial spiritual substance that fills in the cracks and imperfections of everyday life and makes all those overhyped products staring down from supermarket shelves seem ripe, luminous, and even desirable. In a world filled with junk, people have learned to prefer covers to books, images to reality. Don't wrestle with truth–hum the jingle.

Like Whitehead's previous novels, *Apex* makes it clear from the start that Serious Metaphors are at work within its pages. First, of course, there's the "multicultural bandage" designed to "hide the hurt" when actual life cuts too close. Available in a wide variety of hues, "Apex-brand" bandages (as in "the best of civilization, and of course something you could tumble off of, fall fast") reassure people that they're all "flesh-colored," whatever color they happen to be. After all, a splinter is bad enough–you don't need the injury compounded by a sense of difference. In Whitehead's world, everybody is "colored"–by skin, perceptions, talents, whatever.

Then there's the iconographic history of Winthrop, a moderate-size Midwestern town where the protagonist is called in to preside over a renaming contest. Originally called Freedom by its black founders, it was later rechristened by the Winthrop family, after they established their barbed-wire factory (good for keeping some people in and other people out), and now it stands poised to rename itself one more time–either by reverting to its "original" name (as advocated by the black female mayor) or by embracing something high-tech and altogether forward-looking. For example, how does New Prospera grab you? Clearly, Whitehead's argument is that history and identity are constantly being written, and then written again.

The reigning metaphor of *Apex*, however, is the protagonist's stubbed, and now permanently injured, toe. ("In retrospect there was some inevitability tied up in said stubbing, so he came to believe that his toe wanted to be

stubbed for reasons that were unknowable. Unnamable.")
Our onomastic specialist tries to keep his secret pain safe
from scrutiny, only to feel the infection constantly
spreading and the pus continuing to drip, drip beneath the
continually reapplied bandages. Until, of course, he has the
toe amputated and is left limping from the pain (or
memory) that simply won't go away.

As with the founding moment of Winthrop–when the
dreams of Freedom were sold out and renamed to make
the world profitable for barbed wire–human life, for
Whitehead, is characterized by some form of damage.
When people are hurt by one another, or by history, they
try to keep the pain hidden. But they can only pretend for
so long. Eventually, the pain surfaces, and when it does,
there's only one, barely articulate thing left to say:

Ouch.

In previous novels, Whitehead's prose was often
uncontrolled and confusing, especially in its figurative
language. (The opening pages of John Henry Days are a
textbook example of mixed–or even Osterized–
metaphors.) But in *Apex Hides the Hurt*, he seems to have
smoothed out his stylistic inconsistencies. Many passages
are quite funny, especially those describing the ritualized
think sessions and team camps of modern corporate life,
where executives load their classy-looking briefcases with
barbecue implements or roam through the woods in
loincloths crying, "I am an original hunter! I am an original
hunter!" These corporate honchos and honchettes don't
do their jobs so much as perform them, even when the
only audience worth impressing is themselves.

Still, the prose goes wobbly on occasion, and readers
may find themselves getting lost in scenes such as the
following, when the protagonist decides, after a lonely
dinner in his room, to call it "cocktail hour":

> … Outside the bar, the lobby was busy with talk
> of names and how many nights, as tired pilgrims

leaned at reception to deliver credit cards to the world of incidental charges. The quiet of the previous night was at an end. No more fretful scanning for the horizon; this ghost ship had found the shipping lanes again. There were six other patrons. They sipped and squeezed limes into their drinks and commented on the accommodations and the journey. Talking about details, giving them a hearing, helped tame the loss of beloved routine. Someone asked, "What time is it there?" The slang of everyday exile, of in-between places like airports and hotel bars.

The disconnected, abstract phrases make it hard to follow the simplest syntactical relationships between subject and object, or pronoun and referent. For example, who is "scanning for the horizon" in this scene? Is it the "ghost ship" or somebody looking to find it? And where did the "ghost ship" come from, anyway? Does it comprise the latest influx of residents, or is it the "ship" of commerce, or the "ship" of the mighty hotel? And while we're at it, how do you give a "hearing" to "details"? Readers may not have time to consider Whitehead's most compelling arguments; they'll be too busy trying to figure out where they are and what's happening to whom.

Whitehead writes novels of ideas–which means his characters often don't act so much as think. And once they've finished thinking, they fade away, taking most of the narrative momentum with them. In the concluding pages of *Apex*, we never really learn what happens to the nomenclature consultant or what decision he reaches about renaming Winthrop. Instead, he undergoes a series of half-realizations dressed up as epiphanies, until he concludes that the naming of places is never as important as the always-human struggle to speak their meaning into existence. The act of naming, Whitehead suggests, isn't any sort of lasting achievement, or a means of hammering

155

permanence into things, people, politics, or locations on a
map. Rather, it's the continually imperfect effort we all
make, every day of our lives, to grant sense and
significance to the world, whether the world deserves it or
not. By the end of this short, intriguing, and sometimes
aimless novel, it is hard to dispute an argument filled with
so much intelligence and compassion; but it is equally hard
to feel much concern for the nameless character who
delivers it.

Bookforum – 2006

xi. J.G. Ballard

Review of Kingdom Come

NOBODY EVER HATED the contemporary world with as much intensity and conviction as J. G. Ballard. In five decades of unforgiving literary production, he drowned it, scorched it, flayed it with whirlwinds, deluged it with Martian sand, even transformed it into a crystalline jungle populated by jewel-skinned crocodiles, people and parrots. His characters have been sodomized in car crashes, driven crazy by scientific researchers, hounded by billboards and forced to observe atrocities looping endlessly on movie screens until even Zapruder's exploding bullets seemed as mundane and predictable as elevator music. For Ballard, who died in 2009 at the age of 78, the true horrors of our collective future don't concern what might happen hundreds of years from now in a spaceship; rather, they reverberate in the very ordinary now-ness of freeway overpasses, sports stadiums, high-rise apartment complexes and gated communities. In other words, don't bother watching out for zombies or mutant beasts or whatever. The ones you really need to watch out for are those mall-walkers.

In *Kingdom Come* (published in Britain in 2006), Ballard's latest batch of preapocalyptic savages are happily clad in freshly ironed soccer jerseys and getting ready to fight for the only thing they believe in anymore–shopping at the

Metro-Centre, a domed and cathedral-like supermall somewhere off the M25, just west of Heathrow. During the day, they randomly purchase everything from refrigerators and toasters to "reusable cat litter," but when nighttime comes and the doors silently slide shut behind them, they go elsewhere for action: beating up Asian shopkeepers, attending sports matches, drinking high-octane lagers around the indoor swimming pools of franchise hotels, and watching their own product testimonials on the Metro-Centre's privately operated cable channel–which, in the evenings at least, enjoys "higher ratings than BBC2." But then, BBC2 is part of the old order, while the Metro-Centre is a glorious harbinger of the new one.

Like most of Ballard's late-era novels, from *Cocaine Nights* (1996) through *Millennium People* (2003), *Kingdom Come* is framed as a mystery, but the eventual solution isn't quite so satisfying or precise as what you'd expect from Agatha Christie or Rex Stout. The protagonist–a typically shut-down, middle-class Ballardian antihero named Richard Pearson–goes looking for the killer of his estranged father (who was shot, perhaps assassinated, while buying tobacco at the Metro-Centre), but uncovers nothing more surprising than the serially bland, well-fed faces of other shut-down, middle-class professionals like himself. There's the attractive female cop, trying to keep a lid on the crowds of leaderless consumers; a charismatic, lipsticked and deeply suntanned television host, "the Wat Tyler of cable TV, leading a new peasants' revolt"; a burly lawyer, Geoffrey Fairfax, who sees the Metro-Centre as an invading beast roiling up from the lower orders. Before the mega-mall, Fairfax recalls, "we had a real community, not just a population of cash tills. Now it's gone, vanished overnight when that money-factory opened. We're swamped by outsiders, thousands of them with nothing larger on their minds than the next bargain sale. For them, Brooklands is little more than a car park." Even the otherwise respectable apartment of Pearson's dead father, a retired airline pilot, reveals tidy stacks of literature about Nazis, Mussolini and the BNP. To solve the mystery of suburban violence, Pearson gradually realizes, you don't need to find out who's causing it; it's more a matter of who isn't.

As a local teacher who witnessed the shooting explains, middle-class professionals need to change with the times and "prepare our kids for a new kind of society. There's no point in telling them about parliamentary democracy, the church or the monarchy. The old ideas of citizenship you and I were brought up with are really rather selfish. All that emphasis on individual rights, habeas corpus, freedom of the one against the many… What's the point of free speech if you have nothing to say?" On the other hand: "Consumerism is a collective enterprise. People here want to share and celebrate, they want to come together. When we go shopping we take part in a collective ritual of affirmation."

As you might suspect, there's a lot of irony in Ballard. If his late (and very funny) books sound peculiar to American ears, it's probably because of his very English tendency to play almost everything he says, however outrageous, at moderate to low volume. Unlike the noisier, New Yorkerish avant-garde types who like to shock and awe their readers, Ballard doesn't shout or swear or get in your face. Even his most disturbing obscenities–the porn film sequence in *Cocaine Nights*, say, or the endlessly salacious car-sex scenarios in his unforgettable 1973 novel *Crash*–are as mannered and concise and unimpassioned as a GPS device's soothing, digitally modulated voice describing how to reach the next gas station. (Excuse me– maybe that should read "petrol station.")

Ultimately, the Metro-Centre's new and improved, radically futurized citizenry do what most Ballardian characters do: hunker down in their prisons and embrace their chains, take themselves hostage and refuse to be set free, secretly conspire with their victimizers and worship just about anybody who comes along to tell them how. This is where the future really happens, Ballard reminds his readers–way out in the suburbs where everybody looks like everybody else or faces the consequences. As the bullet-headed psychiatrist, Dr. Maxted, explains (just before he tries to lock the narrator into his asylum): "This isn't Islington or South Ken. There are no town halls or assembly rooms. We like prosperity filtered through car and appliance sales. We like roads that lead past airports, we like air-freight offices and rent-a-van forecourts, we like impulse-buy holidays to anywhere that takes our fancy. We're the citizens of the shopping mall and the marina, the Internet and cable TV. We like it here, and we're in no hurry for you to join us."

PEARSON IS LIKE many of Ballard's protagonists, the ironic, semi-detached observers of cataclysms, who don't feel any personal investment in either the normal order of things or their obliteration by random apocalypses. In some ways, they all hark back to Jim, the autobiographical character in *Empire of the Sun*, wheeling around his prison camp observing the sorrows of people who don't seem to know how lucky they are. Because in Ballard's universe– which patiently assembled itself over decades of remarkable novels and stories and essays–words like "atrocity," "disaster," "terminal" and "catastrophe" aren't necessarily bad. Things could be worse, and the world as we know it might never change at all. Or, as Pearson remarks late in the novel, "Think of the future as a cable TV program going on forever."

You always got there way ahead of us, guy.

J.G. Ballard, you will be missed.

The New York Times Book Review–2012

III.

Past Pleasure Perfect

The Slob Aesthetics of P.J. O'Rourke

IN *PARLIAMENT OF Whores*, P.J. O'Rourke convincingly argues that the problem with American politics today is that it's boring. He goes on to say that the "idea seems to be to make the election of a president so complicated and annoying that no one with an important job or serious avocation–that is, no one presently making any substantial contribution to society–would be tempted to run for office. So far, it's worked." If America's politicians were even remotely interesting, they might at least be able to misrepresent themselves with vigor and imagination. For example:

> Why send yours truly to Capitol Hill, and I'll ship the swag home in boxcar lots. You'll be paving the roads with bacon around here when I get done shoveling out the pork barrel. There'll be government jobs for your dog... You'll get unemployment for the sixteen hours every day you're not at your job, full disability checks if you have to get up in the night to take a leak, and Social Security checks will come in the mail not just when you retire at sixty-five but when you retire each night to bed... Vote for me, folks, and you'll be farting through silk."

Since the late Seventies, P.J. O'Rourke has been one of the leading exponents of what can only be called the Slob School of American Comedy. Most of the Slobs were originally published in *National Lampoon*, where O'Rourke himself was once editor. It began as middle-class male college-kid humor; many of the writers attended Harvard or Yale, and O'Rourke himself graduated from Johns Hopkins. Since *National Lampoon* was not readily available in Europe, most Brits have only experienced Slob Comedy second-hand through such films as *National Lampoon's Animal House*. Some of the humor translates; some of it doesn't.

THE PREMISE OF Slob Comedy is simple. You start with a Slob who is either egregiously drunk or coked to the gills. In O'Rourke's books, as in those of *primum slobus* Hunter S. Thompson, the Slob is characteristically a spoiled white college graduate who likes under-age girls, rolling pick-up trucks, imbibing rude drugs, and crashing loud parties. Most of all, though, he enjoys trashing Phonies. In early Slob Comedy, the Phonies were morally upright Wimps with trust funds, but in Parliament of Whores they have been transmogrified into the scourge of good Republicans everywhere, Liberal Democrats. Like College Wimps, the Liberal Democrats are children of the "old rich;" they have lots of money they didn't earn for themselves, and they take life much too seriously.

Even at its most ruthless, Slob Comedy can be extremely funny–and there are passages in O'Rourke, particularly in *Republican Party Reptile* and *Holidays in Hell*, where you will laugh your shorts off. Slob Comedy sends you laughing in all directions at once. First, it allows you to enjoy cruel, bigoted, sexist jokes without having to take responsibility for them. And if that's not enough, you can simultaneously laugh at the Slob himself because, well, after all, he's a slob. Slob Comedy is irony without a net, and at its best it performs a sort of weird catharsis. The reader feels superior to who he was before he heard these nasty jokes, since he certainly wouldn't run around saying them in public (or at least anywhere he might be overheard by his wife or girlfriend). And the writer gets to feel superior because not only does he get to say these awful things in public, he actually gets paid for it.

When Slob Comedy goes political, for example, you can expect someone like O'Rourke to explain that the American public doesn't give "a hoot" about the Iran-Contra scandal because the "Iranians didn't fire those missiles at anything but other hankie-heads, and Contra graft was used to kill Communists or people who would have become Communists if they'd lived to adulthood."

As readers, we have a good old time laughing at what racist insensitive Yahoos those Americans can be. The threat to a joke like this, however, is when we find ourselves starting to laugh not only at the Slobs, but at all those "hankieheads" who got themselves blown up with overpriced American weaponry, along with those Communists Phonies who were so stupid they got themselves shot by dope-peddling Contras (women and children included–what boobs!) *Parliament of Whores* offers a significant added danger. We begin to feel that there's a good chance the author is laughing at us for giving a good goddamn one way or the other.

The problem with Slob Comedy is that it is essentially elitist, with a weird dash of democracy thrown in. Slob Comedy takes for granted that everybody is democratically jerkish. But while the Slob is a jerk, he's a much more authentic jerk than all the other jerks–the ugly fat girls, welfare-jockeys and pampered Liberals who moan so telegenically about poverty, war, depleting ozone-layers and high-fiber cereals. Unlike the Phonies, the Slob knows how to stop worrying and have fun, and eventually triumphs in all the things only Slobs care about (though if the Phonies weren't so phony, they'd admit caring about them too). The moral of Slob Comedy is this: "Okay, I may be a Slob. But at least I've got all the money, all the girls, and meanwhile–you're still boring!" Think of Rodney Dangerfield in Caddyshack–Slob as apotheosis.

In *Parliament of Whores*, Slob Comedy has adopted a sports coat, a house in the country, a two-car garage, and much too much covert "moral philosophy." First of all, it pretends not to contain any moral philosophy at all, which is, of course, one of the chief assumptions of all moral philosophies. Like the Republican Party, it pretends to be nothing more than good old-fashioned American know-how and common sense. There is even a series of self-congratulatory riffs in which O'Rourke informs us that he used to be a hippy (but wised up) he used to be some sort of leftist (but wised up) and that when he was a kid, he didn't know how poor he really was (unlike all those yokels begging for government handouts). There are times when P.J. O'Rourke sounds less and less like a drug-crazed Republican reptile from hell, and more and more like my grandmother.

In his acknowledgements, O'Rourke apologizes that his statistics and information may be inaccurate, which they often are. But O'Rourke doesn't feel he has to worry too much about numbers, because he claims his humor is more "truthful than factual." (You can always tell when a humorist starts taking himself too seriously—he starts belaboring the inherent "truth" of comedy.) This means that while P.J. Is telling a lot of funny, nasty jokes about crack-addicts and Third World losers, his journalistic information will be salted with some real whoppers. If these whoppers were designed to make us laugh, we might excuse them; but instead they are designed to prove to us that O'Rourke is "truthfully" correct, while everybody else is either "halfeducated," or a "professional bedwetter."

IN *PARLIAMENT OF Whores*, O'Rourke's comedy isn't the grand bloody shoot-'em-up Western it used to be. Instead, it regurgitates a lot of stale, contrived facts and propaganda that right-wing politicians have been hauling out of their briefcases for years. For example, O'Rourke implies that the only people who attend pro-housing demonstrations actually have homes, and that homeless people would rather take charity than work for a living; in fact, the truly homeless are all too insane, drug-crazed and incompetent to speak for themselves. As if that's not enough, figures on the homeless have all been blown out of proportion–P.J. knows this because he checked in with (guess who?) the federal government. P.J. doesn't like the incompetent federal government, but when he needs misleading statistics and they've got what he's looking for, they're nifty.

According to P.J., all this brouhaha about environmental deterioration is nonsense promoted by "doombusters," because the science page of the New York Times said, "most dire predictions about global warming are being toned down by many experts." And by the way, cutting defense spending couldn't do anything substantial to decrease the federal deficit–so leave all those great guns and boats alone. Reading *Parliament of Whores*, you keep coming across opinions that look like jokes, that're structured like jokes, but that aren't funny. Again and again you have to remind yourself, "Uh-oh. I think P.J.'s being truthful again."

There's nothing wrong with a humorist being nasty, dishonest, presumptuous, smug or partisan, but there's something about *Parliament of Whores* that smells. The book feels deeply defensive. It does not simply seek to be funny; it seeks to prove itself right. As a result the reader begins to feel he is engaged in a political complicity he did not bargain for. To some extent, this is O'Rourke's main point. We are all bound up in the same hypocrisy. Suddenly, O'Rourke's perilously thin and deflated moral philosophy catches up with us. We are all whores, he proclaims at the conclusion of this book; we are all democratically self-interested and grabby. The great thing about free enterprise is that the most efficient whores are running the ship. P.J. is extending the same old Slob Comedy geopolitically: the one who wins the game is always the biggest, most self-consciously slobby Slob of all. The rest of us play self-righteous about how awful Slobs are, but we are the Slobs, and not the best of them either.

O'Rourke is funny, intelligent, and at times—such as when he describes a police raid on crack houses in Washington DC—he writes beautifully. But unlike his earlier books, *Parliament of Whores* leaves a bad taste in the mouth; it almost works, but then finally it doesn't work at all. Even if a reader was willing to believe that we're all whores (and I, for one, don't believe this glib bit of Slob-ethics for one minute) the same reader would have to admit that some whores are smellier, uglier, stupider and more dishonest than all the other whores put together. And the smelliest of these whores may even be the ones P.J. has been voting for.

(London) Independent, 1991

The Story of Art Pepper

STRAIGHT LIFE IS the autobiography of a man who
never understood anything but his own talent. Born in Los
Angeles in 1925, Pepper was raised by a longshoreman
father who beat him, an alcoholic mother who enjoyed
getting him stoned, and an excessively stoic grandmother
incapable of showing any sort of human affection. He
went on to become the greatest jazz saxophonist of his
generation.

His style and range encompassed the smooth
companionable shifts of Lester Young, the glittery nervy
bebop of Bird, and the weird, often interstellar flights of
Coltrane and Coleman. When Pepper played, he took trips;
and when audiences listened, there were times when they
thought he might never find his way back again. He always
did, though. Musically, that is.

But once the music stopped, Pepper began looking for
other ways to get high, and unfortunately he found them.
Booze, marijuana, nicotine, cough syrup, nutmeg, sex with
groupies, insecticide, morphine, Dilantin, Percodan,
Phenobarbitol, you name it. While performing with the
Stan Kenton band in Chicago in 1950, Pepper was
introduced to heroin. It immediately brought him, he
claims, "this peace like a kind of warmth." And when he
examined his reflected eyes in the bathroom mirror, "it
was like looking into a whole universe of joy and
happiness and contentment... I loved myself, everything
about myself... I looked at myself in the mirror and I
looked at Sheila and I looked at the few remaining lines of

heroin and I took the dollar bill and horned the rest of them down. I said: 'This is it. This is the only answer for me. If this is what it takes, then this is what I'm going to do, whatever dues I have to pay…'"

Pepper accepts a strange, almost obsessive responsibility for his life, perhaps because, like many addicts, he's something of an egomaniac. He can't bear to think there are forces beyond his control that might be shaping his life; instead, he believes he's a force that happens to everybody else.

"I believe I'm above anybody I meet," Pepper confesses. "Anybody. Everybody. I think that I'm more intelligent—innate intelligence; I feel that I'm more emotional, more sensitive, the greatest lover, the greatest musician; I feel that if I had been a ball player I'd have been in the Hall of Fame. There's no question in my mind: if I ever became crazy I would probably be Jesus. But, unfortunately, I've never been crazy. I've just been totally sane."

The first "Return of Art Pepper" occurred in 1960, after two short terms in prison and a longer, sustained one of self-abuse. At this time, Pepper began recording again and claims that, out of a deep sense of dissatisfaction with his life, he decided "to get really far out and having everything change, and in order to do that I started using just a ridiculous amount of heroin. And so I put myself in a position where I was no longer able to function, really where it became obvious to everyone what was happening… They thought this was something that was happening to me, that I had no control over. But I was doing it. Purposely. Purposely doing it for some end that I'm not really sure what it was except that I knew I wasn't happy in this false paradise I had carved out for myself in Studio City."

These "purposeful" acts of uncomprehending self-destruction led him into two periods of incarceration at San Quentin, where Pepper found a weird sense of fulfillment and happiness. He quickly made friends with the other convicts because he was "right. That's the only criteria. If you're right, not a rat. If you're a regular; if you're righteous people; if you haven't hurt anyone; if you haven't been rank to people; if you haven't balled some guy's old lady when he went away. Word filters through."

In this inverted paradise, Art Pepper spent his weekends "playing music, reading, and trying to get loaded." Perhaps he felt content because he didn't have as much time or opportunity to destroy himself anymore; in fact, at this point there wasn't that much self left to destroy.

PEPPER BEGAN HIS professional career at the age of 17 with Benny Carter, and quickly became associated with what was known as "West Coast Cool," a more laid-back, less-beboppy style percolating up from LA's Central Avenue. In 1951, the *Down Beat* jazz poll placed Pepper's alto second only to Charlie Parker, and only by a slim margin.

As usual in his life, whenever things started looking really good, Pepper began behaving really bad. He spent eleven of the next sixteen years in prison, intermittently creating more than his fair share of brilliant albums with his avuncular record producer, Les Koenig–most notably *Smack Up!* and *Art Pepper Meets the Rhythm Section*. According to magazine interviews (many of them reproduced in this book) Pepper was continually in the process of rehabilitation, but this was usually just a con he played to satisfy the squares. After a long flirtation with Synanon, the addict-run rehab organization in Los Angeles, Pepper left when they tried to make him quit cigarettes. Then he took a job in a bakery, and tried the State's methadone program for a while.

He announced his second "return" in the mid-70s and produced, again with Koenig, what for my money are the finest jazz albums ever recorded. *Living Legend*, *The Trip* and *Winter Moon* display Pepper's greatest gifts–long unraveling emotional waves of melody and riff. They take you on journeys. But when they bring you home again you're never certain it's a place you've been before.

Pepper produced two different types of music. One was his bop, which unnerved me, like the crackling chemical let-down of an amphetamine rush or a sleepless weekend. It's the edge and circumlocution you find in the more hyperactive passages of Pepper's autobiography–a white Californian trying to be Bird. On the other hand, there are the ballads–"Ophelia," say, or "Our Song." For me, this will always be the real Pepper, playing what he felt when nobody was listening: the swelling, mournful, incommensurable stuff of him, modulated and informed by technique, but pure emotion nevertheless. Unlike his bop, Pepper's ballads leave you feeling illuminated, not simply intoxicated.

In the tradition of Mezz Mezzrow's *Really the Blues*, *Straight Life* is an "oral history" about one of the vainest and most eccentric of modern artists. Transcribing a series of interviews with Pepper, his family, and his fellow musicians, it is absorbing for the reason that real voices are absorbing–resounding with as much dissonance as harmony, as much blank incomprehension as total recall. Art Pepper was insecure, cowardly, dishonest, egotistical and self-infatuated–but he tries to tell the truth as he remembers it, and there's not much more you can ask of any autobiographer.

Pepper died in 1982 after doing more abuse to his body than any one book could ever detail. His liver deteriorated, his spleen ruptured, his skin was flayed by cheap tattoos, and eventually he suffered a fatal heart attack at 57. In the mid to late 1970s I regularly went to see him perform at *Donte's* in the San Fernando Valley, and he looked like someone who had been dry-cleaned a few times too often. But his music was always beautiful, evolving, progressive, never the same from one night to another, and sustained by a sense that this man was producing the best that was in him–even if the way he lived wasn't making him friends.

I was pretty young at the time, and while I was drawn by and (I hope) recognized his talent, I know his story attracted me a little bit too. I had a lot of conventionally adolescent ideas back then–about the criminal artist and all that nonsense that leads us to admire bad Beat poetry or Norman Mailer's self-congratulatory ravings. Sitting in *Donte's* and listening to Art Pepper, there were times when I felt I was closing in on some sort of personal mythology. I imagined something was happening here that was more important, or more cerebral than mere music.

But of course, if you're lucky, you learn two important things as you grow older.

Mythology is always bullshit. And all that really matters is the music.

(London) Independent, 1992

And Where Might That Be Now, Tom? Remembering Thomas M. Disch

I JUST LEARNED that Tom Disch, one of America's funniest and most entertaining novelists and short story writers, died in New York a few days ago. I was extremely fond of Tom, who I met in 1990, when he was one of the first writers I invited to UCONN for a Visiting Writers series I had just started; and ever since discovering his work as a thirteen year old science fiction fan in the late sixties, I have always been amazed by his productivity, his energy, and his creative joy. The first thing of his that I read was his first paperback original novel, *The Genocides*, in which an awful middle-American family is casually decimated by a mindless alien race; not surprisingly, in Tom's version of the universe anyway, the mindless alien race triumphs, and the awful family just does as it should do—dies horribly. Tom's biggest obstacle in life was probably the intrepid stupidity of science fiction fans and literary critics, who simply didn't get him. He annoyed people, as writers are supposed to do; and obstreperously set about upsetting all those boring unexamined assumptions that clog our minds and media—about the genres he loved, the religions he loathed, and even the literary lions he didn't feel should be lionized. (One of his funniest essay titles was "Our Embarrassing Ancestor: Edgar Allan Poe.") To this day, the boring people who spend their time in London and New York foraging for reputations offered him nothing but blithe disregard. It made him irritable; he often got caught up in pointless vendettas against people who cared for him; and, as a result, he wasn't always an easy person to correspond with, or to speak with on the phone. In person, however, Tom was always all charm.

He was large, loud, quick, funny, honest, and thrilled by any form of attention. On several occasions, when I had him out for repeat guest appearances at UCONN, he delighted everybody he met. On one particularly memorable visit, he performed his one-act theatrical monologue in iambic pentameter, "The Cardinal Detoxes," wearing a wide grey fedora and emoting like mad. This play constituted one of his many verbal assaults on religion, and for a while, he enjoyed (thoroughly) the sudden notoriety of having his play shut down by the Archdiocese of New York. On another occasion, he snored so loud in my guest bedroom that one of the wide-open windows slammed shut with a titanic crash. And every time we met, he talked beautifully and enthusiastically about books and art and music, and listened just as hard. Those of us who enjoyed his company when Tom was Tom were very lucky indeed.

I particularly remember those thick brilliant narratively-rapturous late horror-ish novels about those diabolical creatures of our world that Tom really feared: priests, substitute teachers, doctors, salesmen and, of course, Santa Claus. Then there were the vigorously intelligent and absorbing and always surprising stories: "Casablanca," in which elderly tourists wander through a post-war landscape as vaguely and unresponsively as, well, tourists, snapping endless photos in a foreign land that never seems to surprise them; or "Fun With Your New Head," a hyper-ebullient sales patter hawking that most intimately-irreplaceable item of designer apparel. (Tom worked on Madison Avenue for a few months way back in the sixties and, like any writer worth his salt, milked that thin vein of experience for all it was worth.) Then there was the "The Birds," in which a pair of ducks suffer the worst fates our too-human world has to offer–or "The Shadow, " or "The Alien Shore," or "102 H Bombs," or "The Wall Around America"–so many great stories, and almost all of them neglected by the big boring anthologies that teach our high school and university students how not to read.

Unlike the work of most modern writers, Tom's books were good right from the very beginning with all those great titles: *The Businessman: A Tale of Terror*, *The Brave Little Toaster*, *Camp Concentration*, *The Right Way to Figure Plumbing*, *Getting Into Death and Other Stories*, and, my personal favorite, *Here I Am, There You Are, Where Were We.* His books and stories and poems were always thinking faster than you were from the very first sentence to the very last one. And this in a world where most books are too busily rethinking what was already thought better by somebody else.

Tom's books were always excited about going somewhere new, much like Tom. It always amazed me how few people seemed to recognize his abilities and cantankerous talent, but then he didn't always help himself, either. For while he loved the play and performance of almost any genre you could name–sf and fantasy and gothic and horror and mysteries and opera and children's bedtime stories–his work was too good for the boobs and tweenies who mindlessly hid away in them, like troglodytes in caves. Tom had a regal air; he expected to be respected; people, he seemed to think, were supposed to come to him, and he was probably (as usual) right. But I suspect that most of the people who truly loved Tom and understood him best never actually met him. They only needed to read him–and so experience that dependable repeatable sudden thrill of pleasure we all felt when opening up each new story, or essay, or poem by Tom in all his guises: Thomas M Disch, Tom Disch, and even the ornate, publicity-shy Victorianish lady-novelist, Cassandra

Knye.

It wasn't easy being friends with Tom, and many years ago I gave up trying to speak with him on the phone. He was probably the worst phone conversationalist I have ever known–nothing but a dim uninvolved sequence of slow gentle deeply uninterested yesses and okays and well maybes, as if you were always on the verge of being judged or hung up on. When Tom was alone (but never, it seemed to me, when he had company) he was clearly deeply depressed. A few years ago, he lost his long time partner, Charles Naylor; and while Tom continued to produce fine books up until his death, those books continued to be disregarded. And there was talk that he might lose his rent-controlled book-lined apartment in Times Square. He was not ready to be that alone.

HE WAS ONE of the few contemporary genre writers who deserves to be read in a hundred years. Maybe Bradbury, maybe Ballard and Moorcock, maybe Elmore Leonard, and very very maybe Tom Disch. He excelled at verse, essays, nasty and illuminating book reviews, teleplays, screenplays, the first interactive computer novel, children's stories, opera librettos, you name it–roaming through all the sequestrated and self-obsessed literary wonderlands with an axe, chopping everything to bits and putting it back together in ways that pleased him (and, by default, his readers). There will never be another Tom. I know that's something they always say in these quickly written eulogies by admirers and friends, but really, there never will be. We deserved to keep him longer.

Those who haven't read Tom should try *The Priest: A Gothic Romance*, his best and most completely successful novel. And any collection of his short stories—he was easily one of the best and most inventive story writers of his generation. His very critical books on contemporary poetry and science fiction–*The Castle of Indolence*, and *The Stuff Our Dreams Are Made Of*–enraged the practitioners of both. And what can you say about that? Only: Good going, Tom.

I didn't get many letters from Tom over the years, but there are two that I'll always recall with pleasure. When my son was born, he sent us—out of the blue—a huge beagle-sized deer puppet, with the note: *So now you'll learn how to make animals talk just like your dad.* (Tom was the only writer who responded favorably when I sent him early galleys of what I considered my best book, *Animal Planet*.) And just a few years previously, after I wrote to say how sorry I was that his best novel, *The Priest*, had been ignored by so many people, he sent me a brief, self-illustrated post card. It read:

"I blame Knopf, the Catholic Church, and God."

Yes, Tom. Me, too. As usual, you were right.

Fanzine, 2008

The Death of the Author('s Illusions)

I GUESS I had a lot of illusions about being an author when I was young. For instance, I always thought that the idea of authors or critics writing a personal diary column for a major weekly news magazine was inexcusably vulgar. I mean, I've always preferred writers who kept a low profile in their work. I've never enjoyed, for example, writers who wrote autobiographical novels about talented, misunderstood and boozy writers who were writing autobiographical novels about, you guessed it, talented, misunderstood and boozy writers. I believe in Keats's notion of "negative capability." This means an author or critic's ability to repress his or her own voice and self-interest from a work, thus expressing a far nobler and more enduring vision of our sad, capable, often clumsy race as it struggles to endure these rather perilous times of ours. So why have I condescended to write a personal diary column in a British weekly news magazine? I'll explain this as succinctly as I can. I need the dosh.

I like the term "dosh." Dosh is one of the few British terms that I have affected in the past few years since I came to London to be a professional writer. A lot of people think it is very romantic and glamorous–the idea of coming to London to be a professional writer and all. These are, incidentally, people who have never themselves come to London to be professional writers, so I guess we can excuse them for being so monumentally stupid. Having been a professional writer for a few years now, I've learned that most members of my highly glamorous, romantic profession spend an inordinate amount of time thinking about dosh, or moaning about the dosh they don't have. The rest of the time, they use the dosh they do have to purchase a large amount of severely toxic alcoholic beverages. In fact, you might even say that purchasing severely toxic alcoholic beverages and moaning about dosh are activities that occupy a professional writer's free time simultaneously. I guess the old saying still goes: you can never have too much of a good thing.

It probably all seemed pretty romantic when Hemingway, Fitzgerald and that lot were doing it, but they're all dead now, so that shouldn't really matter to any of us. Because writers spend an exceptional amount of their lives in bookstores, they generally feel pretty envious, confronted by the multitudinous books published every year describing how much fun it was being an exiled American writer in Europe in the Twenties and Thirties, going to bullfights, unraveling the lunatic utterances of the intensely dull Gertrude Stein, and partaking in many guilty pleasures which were apparently available to professional writers then but, by the looks of it, are not so readily available now.

WHEN WRITERS AREN'T moaning about dosh or drinking alcohol, they spend the rest of their time waiting for the telephone to ring. Writers spend a lot of time waiting for the telephone to ring for two very important reasons. First, it beats the hell out of writing. Second, there's always the possibility–however remote–that Steven Spielberg has just stumbled across a stray manuscript of your latest unpublishable novel or short story and wants to option it for $200 million, fly you to Hollywood, introduce you to an unimaginably trashy series of gross and unilluminating physical encounters with a wide variety of busty, ambitious young starlets, and ruthlessly corrupt your aesthetic purity.

Aesthetic purity is the quality most writers apply to

themselves whenever they aren't having any fun, or they aren't earning any dosh. Aesthetic purity is also the very first thing most writers will enthusiastically jettison like mismatched furniture whenever confronted by even the remotest possibility that they could be joyously corrupted by Hollywood. Admittedly, the odds of a phone call from Steven Spielberg in the lives of most writers are pretty slim. But, as any good writer will tell you, that's still a hell of a lot better than no odds at all.

DOSH, ALCOHOL, WAITING for the telephone to ring, and aesthetic purity were not mentioned in any of the professional writer's trainee manuals I remember reading when I was young. Instead, most of these manuals talked a lot about double-spacing and self-addressed stamped envelopes. They talked about snappy dialogue, point of view, plot development, and characterization. They talked about cover letters, mixed metaphors, and the proper way to affix strong durable paperclips to heavy white bond paper. Any professional writer worth his or her salt will tell you not to worry too much about any of these things. Minor technicalities such as plot development and characterization are mere distractions compared to the professional writer's primary concern, which is, of course, getting paid. Getting paid occupies the writer's thoughts and time in a way that make all the minor inconveniences involved in producing good writing seem pretty dull and uninteresting by comparison.

Getting paid involves periodically calling a number of faceless, malign people on the telephone who work in dark, labyrinthine places known as Accounting, Books, Records, and so on. Most of these faceless people are paid a substantial sum of money to avoid paying freelance writers their fair share of dosh on a regular basis. I'm sure these faceless people have other important duties on their minds as well, but not paying freelance writers must be one of their primary concerns, if only because they do it so well.

WRITING MAY WELL be the only profession where time is graphed and measured according to events that haven't happened. The work that hasn't been sold, published, paid for, reviewed, promoted, read, appreciated, or adapted for television. Things that haven't happened, incidentally, is the principal topic of conversation whenever writers get together. Sitting with a bunch of drunk, impoverished writers and hearing them tell you about what hasn't happened for them, and how much dosh they haven't been paid, and who hasn't rung them on the telephone is one of the most miserably depressing ways imaginable to spend an evening.

And this, of course, is why most writers prefer to drink alone.

The Listener, 1989

When I'm in Santa Barbara

LET'S SEE HOW much of this I've got straight. There are these two old families, living in Santa Barbara, who've loved and hated one another for generations–the Capwells and the Lockridges. Then there's a sort of subsidiary, working-class family, who, of course, don't really matter much except to provide more suspects when people get murdered, and general metaphysical distress.

Joe loves Kelly, who hates Joe because he killed (she thinks) her brother, Channing Capwell. C.C. Capwell hates his son Mason because Mason (he thinks) killed his son, Channing Capwell. Mason, Channing's brother, seems to hate everybody because they didn't kill Channing Capwell, whom Mason seems to have despised, much like everybody else in Santa Barbara. Lionel Lockridge (world-famous anthropologist and traveler) has just returned after some Borneo expedition, and he and his son (Andre? or Martin?) love one another despite the fact each of them thinks the other one killed Channing Capwell.

Meanwhile, Santana, the beautiful daughter of the Capwells' Mexican servants, seems to love every man she can get her hands on; many years ago, she secretly gave birth to a son, Brandon, by Channing, who has subsequently been adopted by some woman who wants to marry C.C. (who, of course, has all the money). Nobody seems to suspect Santana yet of killing Channing Capwell, which, of course, makes her my prime suspect. There's a guy named Peter, a kind of rat-of-all-trades, who's in the hospital dying of some damn thing or another. Everybody thought he killed Channing Capwell, but then they changed their minds. As I understand, Channing Capwell was murdered five years ago. Nobody ever seems to figure anything out very quickly in *Santa Barbara*.

The important thing to remember about *Santa Barbara* is that in America this show lasts for one hour, five days a week, 52 weeks a year. In order to write such a show, it's necessary to be a little redundant from time to time. People don't simply fall in and out of love with one another in *Santa Barbara*. Rather for many weeks and months everybody stands around talking about how two specific people fell in and out of love with one another.

"So John, you mean Santana and C.C. were having an affair, but now they're not anymore?"

"That's right, Jane. C.C. loved Santana. But things didn't work out. I don't know. It really makes you wonder doesn't it?"

"It sure does. I mean, the fact that C.C. and Santana loved each other so much, and now that's all ... you know. It's all over."

"It sure is. It's all over and done with–that's for sure. And now that C.C. and Santana don't love each other, they've had to stop seeing each other as well."

"So do you think they'll get back together? C.C. and Santana, I mean."

"I don't know Jane. I really don't. By the way–did you kill Channing Capwell? Sorry–don't mean to be rude. Go ahead and finish your salad. Just asking, I guess."

I'VE BEEN TO Santa Barbara many times, usually to stop at Denny's for a meal that lasted long enough to allow whatever automobile I was driving to stop overheating so I could resume my latest vagrant trip between L.A. and San Francisco. While my Ford or Chevy steamed and boiled in the parking lot, I would eat my over-medium eggs, hash browns and toast, gaze out of the window through the inverted Denny's insignia and contemplate the blue skies and bluer water. In my many visits to Santa Barbara I have never loved or hated anybody with any particular intensity, nor have I ever once been suspected of murder, rape, financial inveigling, or bad acting. Perhaps I'm being unfair on Santana. Perhaps *I* killed Channing Capwell.

Schlock is America's Parthenon. I mean, a lot of nations manufacture schlock, but only America produces it with enthusiasm. *Santa Barbara* is currently on Thames Television, in excerpted form, on Thursdays and Fridays at 12.30pm. This doesn't necessarily harm *Santa Barbara*'s contents so much as cut down on my quality viewing time. I live, currently, in rather dingy circumstances, and many mornings when I cannot devise an intelligent reason for getting out of bed, I can still convince myself of the merit in reaching beside my bed, activating my miniature television, and watching *Santa Barbara*.

Whenever I watch these exceptionally beautiful people loving and suffering, I feel a calm, enduring faith in the inherent powers of all men and women to transcend their tawdry, uninteresting and usually insolvent lives and become something better–like television actors. Rarely do I have any clear idea who any of these people really are, or what they think about one another. But then, you see, none of that matters–because I'm in *Santa Barbara*.

The world does not always threaten us with the malign, but with the mundane as well. Unpaid bills, unraveling wallpaper, estranged friends and lovers, the long, beatless parade of routine jobs and domestic chores. Only *Santa Barbara* manages to keep this mundane world at bay. Only in *Santa Barbara* do people really hate, really have a good time, really live. Our own lives, by contrast, seem merely like Platonic shadows of these perfect forms, these perfect faces, this photogenic, well-orchestrated and perfect life. Many sober sociologists seem to think television viewers have trouble distinguishing TV drama from real life, but I think that's condescending, as well as inaccurate and rude.

We all know *Santa Barbara* isn't real. That's why we

watch it.

The Listener, 1988

An Alien at the Movies

WHEN I WAS growing up in San Luis Obispo, California, my younger brother and I, and our various friends, used to meet at one another's homes every Friday evening at 8pm and watch *The Science Fiction Movie Theater* on Channel 2. Like most programs designed for children, *The Science Fiction Movie Theater* featured a variety of strange atrocities and tortuous deaths calculated not only to send us horrified and sleepless to our beds, but to leave our imaginations steaming for days with the possibility that, because the word "science" was implicated, these bizarre events might, at any moment, actually happen.

People were clawed to death by aliens aboard their tinny, fluorescent spaceships, drained of blood by bat-like appendages of a pulsating Martian brain, and transformed into doll-sized prisoners by a malevolent, glassy-eyed scientist. In *The Amazing Colossal Man* (perhaps my most vivid childhood memory), a normally patriotic Army colonel was elevated by a freak radioactive accident into a towering, hairless madman who performed a crude version of acupuncture on a normal-sized doctor with a gigantic hypodermic.

Radiation was a very dangerous thing, my friends and I wisely concurred. At one time or another, radiation transformed almost every conceivable species of animal, plant and paramecium into enormous toothy menaces capable of devouring people, automobiles, and even high-rise apartment buildings. This all made a certain amount of subconscious sense to children. Radiation was a threat we had read about in newspapers. Some of us were even observing as our fathers dug holes in the back yard, where they went on to install bomb shelters filled with canned goods, bunk beds and gardening implements. If this radiation deal got out of hand, we were all going to go live in the newly poured outdoor concrete basement. We wouldn't have to go to school ever again; but just as certainly, it would mean an end to blissful weekends just lying on the floor and watching science fiction on TV.

Science-fiction films existed before 1945, but it was the bombing of Hiroshima and Nagasaki that convinced the movie-going public that, in the atomic age, the unconscionable could abruptly become very real indeed. The Cold War year 1950 marked the beginning of the 'boom' in the first large-scale commercial production of SF films, and even a cursory survey of the titles produced during this period describes America's widening anxieties about both science and men. *Giant from the Unknown*, *The Man from Planet X*, *Unknown World*, *When Worlds Collide*, *Invasion USA*, *Zombies of the Stratosphere*, *It! The Terror from Beyond Space*, *This Island Earth*, and *The Night the World Exploded* all reverberated with Fifties alienation and unease. Science was suddenly linked in the popular imagination not with knowledge, but with threat; the universe was no longer something to be explored and made explicable, but rather a brooding and inscrutable presence to be dreaded. "Watch the skies," warned the ominous narrator of Howard Hawkes's *The Thing*. Unless we were careful, the future would arrive at any moment.

Monsters were among us, but that didn't mean they weren't easily identifiable by their preference for books, outlandish contraptions and inhumanly unemotional theories–much like Nazis, Communists and university professors. Unless one was careful, dire "things" and impersonal "its" descended in the night. They were members of alien races; they desired our beautiful human women; and, if that weren't bad enough, almost every one of them was a consummate professional scientist. They knew how to control spaceships and space weapons; they could assemble, activate and deploy vast complex forces capable of destroying entire planets.

Even when these aliens were presumably "good," like the mild-mannered Michael Rennie in *The Day the Earth Stood Still*, or the wobbly, invisible gelid mass in *It Came from Outer Space*, they still weren't taking any nonsense– especially from a bunch of Earth-bound mortals. If it became necessary, they would disconnect the world's electricity, and abscond to the stars with every living man, woman and child in Milwaukee–and don't think they couldn't do it.

AMERICA LIKES PEOPLE who make things work, and don't waste too much time speculating about what those things mean. Science fiction may have "grown up" in the Seventies and Eighties, but only to imagine more dazzling machinery, more cinematic effects, and rubbery aliens with more flamboyant nostrils. Today, the financial success of cinematic SF has resulted in numerous bright, watchable films, but for the most part they are still aimed at the children's toy market, and when adults exit those echoing cinemas, they must feel slightly clammy and nauseous, as if they have inhaled too many sweets. But in my day, there was nothing glamorous, or high-tech, or even commercially sound about science fiction movies. Instead, they were as cheaply made, and as vulgarly presented, as everything else in middle America. They didn't awe you. They made you feel at home.

IN AMERICA DURING the late Fifties and early Sixties, summer film festivals for children were inevitably sponsored by the Parent-Teacher's Association, or PTA, which was staffed by a highly conscientious and almost unimaginably sadistic committee of reputable men and women who went to great pains to select the numerous awful science-fiction movies shown for our weekend amusement. In the late spring it was possible to purchase a booklet of tickets from the local grammar school, which convinced my brother and I that these rather garish, disturbing movies were in some weird way "educational."

I can't remember much more than a few random bits and pieces from these films, for during such "festivals" I spent most of my time in the lobby, where I developed a rather cordial and amorous affection for the girl who sold the popcorn. In my rather cowish manner, I flirted with this girl who sold the popcorn while I purchased my Bon-Bons and Baby Ruths and struggled very sincerely to evade the horrendous spectacles which awaited me back there in the enormous, cathedral-like movie auditorium. Back there in the dark, puny mortals were crushed beneath the spiked, leathery feet of dinosaurs. Volcanoes erupted and planets collided. People died by the thousands, billions and quadrillions–normal everyday types of people, just like you and me. The name of the girl who sold the popcorn, as I recall, was Wendy. I believe Wendy harbored a number of ambitions to become an actress.

Every few minutes or so I would peek through the swing-doors into the glowing cinema and, whenever I glimpsed an abruptly unthreatening bit of exposition–a scientist pointing at theorems on a blackboard, perhaps, or John Agar engaged in chaste kisses with some nameless blonde co-star–I ventured back down the long sloping vertiginous aisle to my sticky velour seat, where my brother awaited my popcorn with a bemused impatience.

"You missed the best part," my brother said, with what I considered, at the time, to be incalculable bravery. "They ripped the guy's face clean off."

"I know," I lied. "I was watching from the aisle."

The Listener, 1989

Bigfoot

WHILE THERE'S A lot we don't know about Bigfoot, his enthusiasts generally agree that he smells terrible, enjoys leaving footprints where people can find them, and frequents the deepest woods of northern California—a region not coincidentally inhabited by marijuana growers and tall-tale-telling lumberjacks. Primitive, hairy, big-buttocked, and benign (except when he kidnaps local women and takes them home to meet the parents), Bigfoot represents an all-natural alternative to megamalls, the Internet, and TV. Oh, and another thing—after thousands of purported sightings, there's still not a single piece of evidence that this wise, benevolent naturist actually exists. Perhaps this is because Bigfoot isn't a creature of the unknown so much as a hypothetical alternative to the world we know too well. And let's face it, these days we can use all the hypothetical alternatives we can get.

Even though Bigfoot hasn't bequeathed a single carcass (or even a fragment of one) to museums, his genealogy dates back to Pliny's *Historia Naturalis* and the first-century AD, when human beings started mapping nations and postulating the bizarre creatures that lived outside them. As Joshua Blu Buhs explains in his smart, wide-ranging, and sometimes humorless book, *Bigfoot: The Life and Times of a Legend*, the "wildman" has long roamed the margins of what cultures call "civilization." When these bearish creatures aren't being used to scare children into behaving, or to justify the slaughter of native populations, they give our tabloids something to write about besides Elvis.

What makes Bigfoot great, Buhs argues, is that such stories allow people to conspire with their own junk culture of urban legends and conspiracy theories. In other words, it's not that people believe what they're told; rather, they enjoy wondering at what might be true, even while recognizing that it might not be. As P. T. Barnum noted in the 1860s, when he made bundles of cash displaying the "What-Is-It" in his traveling circus, "The public appears disposed to be amused even when they are conscious of being deceived." In this case, the What-Is-It turned out to be a large, shave-headed black man, who wore what looks in photographs like a black shag-carpet jumpsuit. In the long run, the What-Is-It wasn't simply a hoax but a sort of placeholder for subsequent sightings of the Abominable Snowman, Sasquatch, and Bigfoot. He represented that half-familiar something that human beings could marvel at while dimly suspecting that somebody might be pulling their leg.

The notion of extraordinary creatures grows more attractive to our collective imagination as the world grows more mundane, predictable, and dull. Well before Bigfoot began stomping his hairy feet in the muddy woods of California, Sir Edmund Hillary's expedition to Mount Everest in 1951 returned with photos of what some claimed was a Yeti's footprint. Many found the possibility of marvelous, huge, apelike creatures wandering the snowy peaks more fascinating than the fact that men had climbed an impossible mountain. The ensuing media blitz made the Yeti a star. Nepal began selling hunting licenses, the *London Daily Mail* dispatched an expedition to hunt down the beast, and Hilary himself led a return trip during which he decided that the Yeti didn't actually exist. The footprints, his team concluded, were formed by sublimated snow, and widely reported Yeti pelts turned out to be bogus. This didn't bother the public, though. Bogus was OK. Sure, it meant that somebody was trying to take advantage of their belief in the marvelous. But the more convincingly these marvelous events were discredited, the more people reported them, and the more they were reported, the more they were believed. Go figure.

The Yeti became known as the Abominable Snowman, and as the Abominable Snowman became harder and more costly to find, it moved to the Canadian wilderness and became known as Sasquatch, darker and stronger and prone to meddling with heavy machinery. Tabloid stories begat tabloid stories, and eventually the creature moved down to northern California, where it inspired the building-contractor brothers Ray and Wilbur "Shorty" Wallace. Big footprints began showing up throughout Humboldt County, construction equipment was found vandalized, and Ray's sightings grew so frequent, bizarre, and unbelievable that people tended to believe him, even when he claimed to have captured a Bigfoot baby, and kept it alive on nothing but Kellogg's Frosted Flakes. Most didn't find these reports funny; they took them as evidence that the world was a lot more interesting than it seemed. Journalists and filmmakers began prowling the area and spending their money in local diners and motels; scientists, academics, and big-game hunters came looking for the missing link, tenure-worthy subjects for their next scholarly article, and trophies for their living-room walls. As one of Ray's close friends, Rant Mullens, later declared, "These higher educated guys are dumber than anybody."

In 1957, Tom Slick, cofounder of Slick Airways and a friend of Howard Hughes, mounted an expedition in search of the Abominable Snowman, but when he ran into trouble in Nepal, he transferred the whole shebang to California, where his forest-roving band of peculiarity-seekers nailed soiled sanitary napkins to trees (Bigfoot was reputedly fond of human females) and pawed through animal droppings. George Haas, a warlock, gardener, and sci-fi fan from Oakland, began publishing the *Bigfoot Bulletin* in 1969 in order to stay in contact with other serious *afficionados*; in two years, circulation of the newsletter hit three hundred.

By the late '60s and early '70s, it became increasingly difficult to tell the scientists apart from the crazies. Take Grover Krantz, who staged "scientific experiments" that consisted of wearing prosthetic brow ridges in order to better relate with Homo erectus. A faculty member at Washington State University who liked to compare himself to Sherlock Holmes and Leonardo da Vinci, Krantz published an academic paper on Bigfoot's posture based solely on footprints that someone claimed belonged to a beast that nobody had ever captured. Krantz helped create a new academic field: cryptozoology, the search for and study of legendary animals.

Then there was Roger Patterson, author of *Do Abominable Snowmen of America Really Exist?* (Guess what he decided by the end of his deep research into the question? They *do*!) A former acrobat and rodeo performer, Patterson captured a Bigfoot on twenty-four feet of celluloid, a film that resembles a preliminary sketch for *The Blair Witch Project*. In this remarkably mundane piece of cinematic history, a Bigfoot female strides casually through Bluff Creek, California, pauses to glance over her shoulder, and strolls off into the woods. Patterson first screened this brief encounter at the University of British Columbia in 1967 and then allowed the clip to be incorporated into a feature-length "scientific" film, which sold ten thousand tickets in two showings at its premiere in Spokane, Washington. Like the Zapruder film, this clip has been shown so many times that it's taken on a reality of its own.

As Michael McLeod decides in *Anatomy of a Beast*, his funny, well-written memoir about chasing down the believers, the hardest part about a subject like Bigfoot is trying to separate what *can* be believed from what we *want* to believe. And from the evidence collected so far, what we *want* to believe is pretty preposterous. So until we all visit Bigfoot in a zoo and snap his photo with his hairy, avuncular arm draped around Auntie Marge, we'll have to settle for Bigfoot burgers, Bigfoot rafting, Bigfoot campsites, Bigfoot motels, and Bigfoot miniature golf. The truth is definitely out there, and this is it: You can buy a plaster cast of a nonexistent being's footprint for twenty bucks. Go get it!

Bookforum, 2009

ABOUT THE AUTHOR

Scott Bradfield has spent his entire life reading, and writing, unwisely. He is the author of five novels, three books of short stories, and the forthcoming *Dazzle Resplendent: Adventures of a Misanthropic Dog*. He lives in London and San Luis Obispo.

92847966R00113